Paths of Life

Paths of Life

Daniel Mensah Brande

Paths of Life

© Daniel Mensah Brande 2024

All rights reserved. Without limiting the rights under copyright reserved above, no part of this publication may be reproduced, stored in a retrieval system, or transmitted, in any form or by any means (electronic, mechanical, photocopying, recording or otherwise), without the prior written permission of the copyright owner of this book.

Published by
Lighthouse Christian Publishing
SAN 257-4330
5531 Dufferin Drive
Savage, Minnesota, 55378
United States of America

www.lighthousechristianpublishing.com

Contents

Dedication

Acknowledgments

Introduction

Chapter One: The Joys and Tragedies of a Refugee Family

Chapter Two: Ruth and Orpah at a Glance

Chapter Three: Familiar Path Versus Unfamiliar Path of Faith

Chapter Four: Unfamiliar Path Sees the Glory of God

Chapter Five: Familiar Path Breeds Grasshopper Mentality

Chapter Six: The Mount Horebs on The Unfamiliar Path

Chapter Seven: Unfamiliar Path Subsists on Hard Work

Chapter Eight: The Unshakable Power of Faith-Shepherded Unfamiliar Path

Dedication

To my late mom and dad:

This is your book, a memorial from me to you;
For cultivating an evergreen garden of virtues;
From which, I harvested the virtue of humility;
A universal currency for purchasing anything and everything; Love, peace, patience, forgiveness, self-control, gratitude, and all; Your sublime, heavenly humility, always puts me ahead of the curve; My undying gratitude to you, Mom and Dad, expressively expressed in humility.

Acknowledgments

Conceiving an idea, and turning it into an information format, as a book, is an arduous task, demanding systematic shaping and re-shaping, and meticulous tuning and fine-tuning. So, it was with this book. Every aspect of it was painstakingly massaged, to give it a fascinating and enigmatic look. This was a task beyond my very own capacity. What you are reading is a product of cross-pollination of thoughts. From the idea generation, through the writing, to the production, people from diverse stations of life invested time, knowledge, and energy to midwife this title. And I owe them inexpressible gratitude.

My unbounded gratitude goes to my wife, Gloria Brande; my son, Selasi Mensah-Brande; and my daughter, Emefa Mensah-Brande for giving me the love and prompting I direly needed, to cross the thin line dividing success and failure. Theirs is gratitude beyond compare.

I owe Pastor Daniel Lamptey enduring gratitude for his suggestions that, not only seasoned the book with engaging and entertaining flavors but also made it intellectually stimulating.

Finally, I am highly indebted to the publishers, editors, and cover designers. They provided the delicate finishing, to clothe the book with a venerable personality. I exceedingly acknowledge their contribution, and deservingly honor them with an overwhelming 'thank you.'

Introduction

This is a familiar story in the Bible. It has a wide audience and regularly features sermons, sermonettes, devotionals, and exhortations. And it always appeals to conscience, emotions, imagination, and reason. The suspenseful plot-driven narrative pitches a standout virtue against a perceived vice. As expected in faith-cloned stories intended to illustrate moral and spiritual lessons of evil versus good, virtue triumphs over vice. The virtue here is unalloyed loyalty, while the vice is absolute disloyalty.

The triumph of loyalty elevates the main character in the story, to the summit of human edification while relegating the character associated with disloyalty, to the oblivion of human erudition. The message often gleaned from this tear-jerking story of an economic refugee family, terrorized and tyrannized by deaths and widowhood, colors, and highlights unalloyed loyalty as an indispensable virtue for human subsistence.

However, I have carefully sieved the story, emptied it of the debris of emotions and uninformed conclusions, and reformatted it, to tell a tale of two opposing paths of life: a familiar path set against an unfamiliar path. Whether we are aware of it or not, our destinies are umbilically tied to, and stubbornly controlled by, one of these two paths of life. On our journey of life, we consciously or unconsciously travel on a path we are familiar with or a path that is unfamiliar to us.

On the familiar path journey, we meet familiar people and familiar events. In contrast, the unfamiliar path journey exposes us to unfamiliar people and events. The familiar path, unsurprisingly, takes us to a familiar destination, while the unfamiliar path, unquestionably, lands us at an unfamiliar destination.

Each of the two destinations is a world of its own. The familiar destination has familiar joys and challenges. In the same way, the unfamiliar destination has its joys and challenges, which are not familiar. Similarly, each of the two paths offers its future for its passengers. The future that the familiar-path-bound journey gives its travelers, is entirely different from the future available to travelers on the unfamiliar-path-bound journey. But do we have the slightest inkling of the future installed in these two opposing paths of life? Do we know which of the two parallel paths will shepherd us to realize the true purpose of life?

In an attempt to provide fetching answers to these mind-bending questions, *Paths of Life* takes you on an exciting journey to explore the two worlds of the two paths. During the exploration, *Paths of Life* will assist you in sampling the cultures of the two worlds, and convince you to engage in a frank chat with their inhabitants. At the end of your exploration, you will, unsuspectingly, become either a **Ruthenian** or an **Orpahian**. But who are the **Ruthenians** and **Orpahians**? After flipping through the pages of this faith-infested, soul-stirring book, you will, undoubtedly, know their identities, and opt for membership in one of them.

CHAPTER ONE

The Joys and Tragedies of a Refugee Family

Here is a story of loyalty. Is it rather a tale of two opposing paths? It comes from the holy book of the Christian faith, and it is very interesting. It is a small story with a big message. It recounts how God weaves huge stories out of trivial stories of ordinary people. The emotion-stirring story lays bare the vast potential for greatness installed in every human being but cautions that that greatness could become a disaster if the huge potential is misdirected.

It is a story that encourages us to regard every aspect of our everyday life as a plot of God's bigger story for humanity. The main character in this seeming love story, is a poor, hurting outsider, an outcast, a stranger, who has no entrance to a relationship with God, and no claim to the promises of God. But God has woven her everyday story into His bigger story for her to become an heir to His covenant promises.

The short, rip-roaring narrative is about three men, three deaths, and three widows. And it begins with a couple and their two sons, who fled their native land to escape a severe famine. They found a new home in a foreign land, where food was in abundance. They began a new life as economic refugees and settled down well.

But the religion practiced here was entirely different from theirs. It was a pagan religion, whose worship, their ancestors had warned against. As a result, the refugee family stuck to their homegrown region. But with time, they got used to the people's way of living.

However, tragedy struck the family. The celebrations of a greener pasture had turned into grieving deaths and agonies of widowhood. The greener pasture the family sought had become a cemetery. The man died, and ten years later, his two sons, who had gotten hitched to home-grown sweethearts also died, leaving their widowed mother and their young widows shattered and broken, confused and disappointed. Culturally, women here totally depended on male relatives for their livelihood. Without male relatives, women had no hope and were condemned to the fringes of society.

And this was the fate, that had befallen the three widows: a mother-in-law and her two daughters-in-law. They had no insurance coverage from any male relatives and were living in miserable misery. A moving story of three men, three deaths, and three widows. The three men who, also doubled as the three deaths, were Elimelech, a Bethlehem indigene, and his two sons, Mahlon and Chilion, while the three widows were Elimelech's wife Naomi and her two daughters-in-law, Ruth and Orpah.

Interestingly, the names of the people and places that starred in this harrowing story, had mind-bowling and fascinating meanings:
- Elimelech means *My God is King*

- Naomi means *Sweet*, which was later, changed to Mara, meaning *Bitter*
- Bethlehem, means *House of Food* or *House of Bread*
- Judah means *Praise*
- Moab means *Seed of the Father* or *From My Father*
- Mahlon, the elder son of Elimelech means, *Sick* or *Sickness* or *Sickly*
- Chilion the younger son of Elimelech means *Pining* or *Wasting Away*.
- Ruth means *Friend* or *Compassionate Friend*
- Orpah means *Neck* or *Stiff-Necked* or *Fawn* or *Gazelle-Like*
- Boaz means *Swiftness*

Perhaps, the spirits propelling these amazing names significantly influenced the plots that drove the heart-rending, empathetic story to its surprising apogee. As the biblical story recounts, a devastating famine in Bethlehem in the nation of Judah, forced Elimelech and his family to relocate to Moab, an enemy territory, where food was abounding.

In other words, a ravaging famine drove Mr. *My God is King* and his wife, Madam *Sweet*, and their two sons - *Sickly* and *Wasting Away* - out of their hometown, *House of Food* in the nation of *Praise*, to migrate to *Seed of the Father,* a greenery, fertile valley, just short of the Promised Land, to search for food.

It was a surprising relocation, at the invitation of food, to an enemy territory of Moab, a nation that so envied the numerical strength and military supremacy of Israel that it once engaged the services of a renowned prophet to beg God to curse Israel. Even though, by the dictates of God, the prophet blessed the Israelites instead of cursing them, the Moabites and the Israelites had since shared nothing in common other than enmity. The Moabites were on record as having allied with other nations to rise against the Israelites and subject them to a humiliating defeat.

The Moabites, a distant relative of the Israelites, were the offspring of an incestuous relationship between Lot and the elder of his two daughters. Seeking to preserve their family line, through their father, the two daughters of Lot got their father drunk, and slept with him. The descendants of the younger daughter were the Ammonites, who together with their Moabite cousins, became archenemies of the Israelites.

And instantly, packing bags and baggage from his fruitful **House of Bread** abode, and heading to an enemy territory of **Seed of the Father**, at the request of a famine outbreak, demonstrated the highest point to which Elimelech had betrayed his nation, Judah. It also demonstrated his disloyalty to the very spirit propelling his very name, Elimelech. He seemed to have had no faith in the import of the name and completely abandoned the spirit driving the name. Elimelech failed to exhibit the faith, courage, and patience needed to truly live up to the spirit behind his name **My God is King**.

As a Mr. *My God is King*, Elimelech should have had the faith and patience to wait for his 'God to be the king' to rule over the food crisis in his native land. Instead, he escorted his family, to become economic fugitives in an enemy encampment. Elimelech did not honor his name. He only confessed God as king, with the rendition of his name, but not in the practice of life.

Just as he failed to acknowledge the importance of the meaning of his name, Elimelech also failed to acknowledge the import of the *House of Bread* meaning of his hometown, and the *Praise* meaning of his nation, Judah. Instead of praising God and asking God why there was no bread in the *House of Bread*, Elimelech absconded with his family to an enemy environment to look for bread.

Regrettably, the place where Elimelech thought he and his family would get redemption, was the very place they met calamity. Perhaps, his actions were driven by fear and emotions, not by faith. He lacked faith in his very name **God is King**, in his hometown's name **House of Bread**, in his nation's name **Praise**, and in the name of the **God of Israel.**

One other intriguing, but disappointing background to this mournful story, wrapped up in a double jeopardy of three deaths and three widows, was the self-sentencing and self-condemning names Elimelech and Naomi had given to their two sons. Naming the children, *Sickly*, and *Wasting Away* might have spiritually sentenced the two innocent young men to sickness and waste. No doubt, they became sickly and wasted away in a foreign land without procreating.

The grief-stricken names Elimelech embossed on his two sons, depicted him to be a faithless father, who panicked at the least setback, and lacked, what it takes, to use setbacks as setups, to navigate trying moments. The children's doleful names also portrayed him to be someone, who perceived God to be in the business of meting out sorrow to people. Elimelech might have even interpreted the famine in his homeland as the usual hand of God at work, inflicting havoc on humanity. This explained why he swiftly bolted away, with his family to Moab.

The calamities that visited Elimelech and his family in Moab were undoubtedly, self-inflicted. They were home-grown tragedies. Elimelech should not have gone to Moab of all places, a nation the Lord Himself had listed among Israel's bitter enemies (Psalm 83: 5-8). He should not also have given his two sons, spirit-dumping and hope-dimming names as the word of God affirms in Proverbs 18:2 that, "death and life are in the power of the tongue, and those who love it will eat its fruits." The power behind the damning names stamped on the two sons appeared to have haunted them and prematurely sent them to their graves.

The two sons too, should not have tied the knot with Moabite women. This act was a contravention of a biblical edict in Deuteronomy 7:3-4, debarring Israelites from marrying Moabites. "Do not inter-marry with them [Moabites]. Do not give your daughters to their sons or take their daughters for your sons, for they will turn your children away from following me to serve other gods, and the Lord's anger will burn against you and will quickly destroy you."

As would be expected, Naomi had put all her hopes in her two sons to cater to all her needs and give her joy, after the death of her husband. But the two sons too, too soon, passed away. They died childless after their marriages, not leaving behind anyone to make Naomi respond to a grandma's call. This worrying situation, drove Naomi into inconceivable confusion and profound contemplation, deflating all her future hopes. Hapless, and confused, she decided to change her name from Naomi, meaning **sweetness** to Mara, meaning **bitterness**. Life seemed to have disappointed her. She became very bitter, relegating herself to nothingness. She knew she had reached her cul-de-sac, the dead-end of her life.

 Possibly, the untold mishaps that befell the Elimelech family could be a divine hand of God at work, to achieve God's purpose. This, and other propelling forces in the hallowing narrative, conspired and inspired to create a disturbing world of widowhood for Naomi and her two daughters-in-law.

However, as the three women were enduring the lonesomeness of widowhood, a word reached Naomi that, the famine in her native land had eased and that there was enough for all to eat. So, Naomi decided to go back to her people in Bethlehem. The two widowed daughters-in-law followed her on the homeward journey. Although the young Moabite women were free to marry elsewhere, they refused to do so and stuck to Naomi. However, as the journey proceeded, Naomi turned to Ruth and Orpah and told them to go back to their families.

Naomi knew it would be difficult for the two young Moabite widows, to make a life of their own, in a foreign land, as men in Bethlehem would not be willing to provide food and shelter for widows, who were not their relatives. She advised them not to follow her to Bethlehem, since she would not be able to offer them any hope for their future.

Sweet-Naomi-now-turned-bitter-Mara advised the young Moabite ladies to go back to their Moabite home, and remarry and have children. She explained to them that, she was too old to re-marry, and even if she did, it would be practically impossible for them to wait for her future sons to be ready for marriage.

".... Go back, each of you, to your mother's home. May the Lord show you kindness, as you have shown kindness to your dead husbands and me. May the Lord grant that each of you will find rest in the home of another husband," (Ruth 1:8-9), Naomi pleaded with them.

But the young widows insisted on following her to her hometown. However, upon persuasive pleas, Orpah abandoned the idea of going with Naomi and decided to go back to her people. But Ruth was unyielding in her insistence to follow her mother-in-law, saying:

".... Don't urge me to leave you or turn back from you. Where you go, I will go, and where you stay, I will stay.

Your people will be my people, and your God will be my God. Where you die, I will die, and there will I be buried...." (Ruth 1:16-17).

Consequently, Orpah retreated to her familiar Moabite home, and settled with her family, while Ruth held on to faith, to settle in unfamiliar Bethlehem with her mother-in-law. As the story later reveals, the presence of Ruth in Bethlehem, transmitted a new lease of hope, not only into the life of Naomi but into the nation of Israel and the world at large.

Faith-filled, hard-working Ruth married Boaz, a relative of Naomi, and bore a son called Obed, the future father of Jesse, who would become the father of King David, from whose royal family line, the Messiah, Jesus Christ would be born. Ruth thus became one of the foremothers of Jesus.

This biblical narrative ended, elevating Ruth to the summit of history while demoting Orpah to the oblivion of history. Orpah enjoyed only two mentions in the Bible. And since her departure to her Moabite household, nothing more was said or heard about her in the Bible. In contrast, Ruth enjoyed thirteen mentions in the Bible, while a whole book was dedicated to her in the Bible, making her and Esther the only two women to have their books in the Bible. Ruth is celebrated throughout the Christian world as a woman of great character and an embodiment of positive traits.

CHAPTER TWO

Ruth and Orpah at a Glance

The two young Moabite widows are biblical characters, who regularly feature in sermons and commentaries of pastors and theology scholars. At all times, Ruth is projected as an amazing woman of the Bible: beautiful, faithful, loyal, courageous, kind-hearted, loving, hardworking, compassionate, generous, respectful, selfless, and diligent. For the aggregation of these rare spiritual qualities, Ruth is always recommended as an excellent role model for women striving to lead a godly life.

In stark contrast, Orpah is harshly treated, constantly vilified and labeled as unfaithful and disloyal. It is often said that Ruth passed the litmus test of trust and loyalty, while Orpah woefully failed. Her very name, Orpah, which translates into *neck, stiff-necked, fawn, or gazelle-like*, is often used to depict her as someone with the propensity to fear or run away, and that she abdicated her duty of staying with her aged, loving mother-in-law. Orpah is easily criticized and judged for her perceived unfaithfulness.

However, that conclusion might not be a fair assessment of the character of Orpah. When a closer look is taken at the whole story in context, Orpah's actions would be understood. She was never disloyal to Naomi. Her decision to go back to her family was even an expression of her loyalty to Naomi's promptings, persuasions, and urgings.

In reality, Naomi set out on the journey back home, with her dutiful daughters-in-law Orpah and Ruth in tow. It was in the course of the journey that, the thoughts of the future of the young widows dawned on her. Realizing that she could not secure any future for the two Moabite ladies, she began pleading with them, to return to their families. Naomi made two unsuccessful pleas to the two ladies, to go back to their families. It was only after the third plea that, Orpah conceded to go back to her people.

From this, it can be deduced that Orpah never lacked loyalty. She was loyal to Naomi to the core. Her decision to bow to the instructions of Naomi, and go back to her family, was a demonstration of loyalty, to a peerless degree. Perhaps, what Orpah lacked was the ability to stand firm by her word. Orpah was disloyal to her word, her conviction, but not to Naomi. It was out of obedience, that Orpah accepted to go back to her family. Departing from Naomi must have been heartbreaking for her. The Bible gives a vivid account of the emotional, tear-flowing, farewell ceremony held for her, at which she kissed Naomi, wept loudly, and bade her goodbye (Ruth 1:14).

Perhaps, Orpah was disloyal to Naomi's God, and not to Naomi per se. Young as they were, the two key issues at stake, for the two young Moabite widows, as they followed their mother-in-law, on a journey to an unknown destination, would be their family life and their spiritual life. Relocating to a place they had never been before, they would, understandably, be concerned with the sociocultural environment of the place. They would be concerned with the ability of the environment to create opportunities for them, to re-marry and start a family. They would also be concerned with the religious practice of the place, and how it could help them build an accepted spiritual life, to peacefully live among the natives.

Initially, the two young, widowed Moabites seemed to be only interested in the people in Naomi's hometown. They collectively indicated this, in their response to Naomi's first plea to them, to go back to their families, saying, "No, we will go with you to your people" (Ruth 1:10). They only mentioned "to your people," and didn't say anything about Naomi's God. It was only after the departure of Orpah, when Naomi tried to use the departure, as an incentive to convince Ruth to go back to her people, that Ruth made her famous "your God will be my God" declaration.

This abundantly demonstrated the high level of knowledge and interest Ruth might have had in the God of Israel. However, this level of knowledge and interest seemed lacking in Orpah, as she was not quoted anywhere in the story, mentioning the name of Naomi's God. Ruth was thus, interested in both her family life and her spiritual life, while Orpah was only interested in her family life.

The difference in the attitude of the two sisters-in-law, towards the God of Israel, might be attributed to the depth of knowledge on the workings of the God of Israel, they might have had from their influencers, especially their husbands and their adoring mother-in-law. It appeared

Mahlon had fully discipled his wife, Ruth in the workings of the God of Israel while, Chilion might have not done so for his wife, Orpah. It might also be that, while Ruth availed herself of the opportunities in the father-in-law's house to learn and know about the God of Israel, Orpah did not do so.

And so, Orpah loyally obeyed the instructions of Naomi, and returned to her people in Moab, while Ruth defiantly disobeyed the instructions of Naomi, and followed her to Israel. The two young Moabite widows thus treaded two different paths in life. Orpah trod the familiar path to go back to the familiar Moabite society and the familiar Moabite gods, whereas Ruth treaded the unfamiliar path of faith to go to the unfamiliar Israel and its unfamiliar God.

Some Hebrew interpretations of the Book of Ruth say Orpah and Ruth were sisters, in fact, daughters of the King of Moab. Even more bizarre, is the Jewish historical account that has it, that Orpah re-married a Moabite giant, with whom she bore four giants, one of whom was the famous Goliath. And how incongruous was it that, a few generations on, a son of Orpah, Goliath would challenge the army of Israel and be killed by David, a great-grandson of Ruth!

And so, why would Ruth and Orpah, two sisters-in-law, who had lived under one family roof for years, decide to take paths that would forever separate them? Remember, both were reared in the Moabite culture and might have turned away from paganism to worship their husbands' faith. Both might have known the power, authority, and love of the God of Israel. Both lived under the warmth of an adoring mother-in-law. Both married brothers and enjoyed blissful marriages until the untimely home calls of their husbands. Both grieved the loss of their husband together. Both were childless and felt the psychological trauma associated with childlessness. Both might therefore have different motivations for the different paths they had trod.

For Orpah, treading the familiar path, would not be a difficult decision to take. Here was a young Moabite lady, leaving behind all the trimmings of her native culture, for a foreign wedlock that appeared to have padlocked her future. Widowed in her prime, childless, and with no guarantee of getting a husband in a foreign land, Orpah would, undoubtedly, be motivated to take a familiar homeward path, where a familiar future was in wait. Moreover, her mother-in-law had made it clear to her and her sister-in-law that, it would be impossible to guarantee them a future in a foreign land.

The desire to be a wife and a mother, and babysit and baby-breastfeed, might have weighed heavily on Orpah. She was aware of the negativities and name-calls associated with childlessness. And being familiar with her home turf of Moab, she decided to tread the familiar path, home.

Orpah had the "better the devil you know than the angel you don't" mentality. She was familiar with the Moabite society, the Moabite culture, the Moabite gods, and more importantly, the Moabite men. She might as well, be familiar with a long list of marriage proposals from which she could choose a husband. And anticipating an uncertain future in the unfamiliar home pasture of her mother-in-law, Orpah decided to take the familiar path back to her familiar, Moabite home.

On the other hand, Ruth was propelled by her rare character traits, to tread the unfamiliar path of faith, remain steadfast in the face of great trials, and stay committed to her friend and mentor Naomi. Ruth was humble, and her unalloyed humility made her put the safety and welfare of Naomi over and above all her needs and concerns. She was loyal, and her fierce loyalty made her become Naomi's ride-or-die, willing to do anything and everything for Naomi, even in the face of danger. She was determined, and her resolute determination made her cling to her resolve to follow Naomi, even if she had to put her life on the line for this to happen.

Ruth was kind, and her loving kindness made her practice royal love to sacrifice, to care for Naomi at all times. She was courageous, and her cheerful courage made her overcome rejection and ridicule, to secure a future for herself and her mother-in-law. She was hardworking, and her diligent hard work made her work heartily as unto God and not unto man for applause. Above all, she was faith-filled, and her unwavering faith shepherded her through the wilderness of want, ridicule, and near-rejection to become the great-grandmother of the famous King David of Israel and foremother of Jesus Christ, the Messiah.

Included in the long list of the spiritual qualities propelling Ruth, are compassion, unfailing, devotion, respect, grace, honesty, generosity, wholesomeness, virtue, honor, and integrity. The qualities of Ruth are so sparkling and all-consuming that, they have become a measuring rod for women of godly character. Women without these spiritual qualities of Ruth are deemed to be ruthless (**ruth-less**) i.e., merciless, pitiless, cruel, heartless, hard-hearted, and harsh. If your behavior is devoid of, at least, one of the several character traits of Ruth, you are seen as ruthless.

It was the combination of these sterling qualities that, drove Ruth to make what I call *the Seven Declarations of Commitment* **to Naomi** (Ruth 1:16-17).

- The "Where you go, I will go" declaration was an expression of an unconditional following, a vow to follow Naomi anywhere, anytime, and in any circumstance.
- The "Where you stay, I will stay" declaration was an expression of making Naomi her **home**, where she would receive parental care and support. It implies the renunciation of her Moabite home and Moabite citizenship, committing to Naomi's home and country.
- The "Your people will be my people" declaration was an expression of absolute loyalty that ties her to all Naomi's relations, friends, neighbors, and everyone Naomi calls her people. It implies the renunciation of her people and commitment to Naomi's people.
- The "Your God will be My God" declaration was a renunciation of her Moabite pagan religion and commitment to Naomi's religion.

- The "Where you die, I will die" declaration was an expression of an irreparable attachment to Naomi, to even death.
- The "And there I will be buried" declaration was an expression of a family bond, vowing to become a family member of Naomi and share the same burying place with her.
- The "If even death separates you and me" declaration was an oath-swearing, pledging an umbilical attachment to Naomi, which can only be separated by death.

In the soul-touching story, we were told that Orpah kissed Naomi, while Ruth clung to her. And so, what kind of kiss did Orpah offer to her mother-in-law? The first kiss recorded in the Bible was between a father and son, Isaac and Jacob-disguised-Esau (Genesis 27:26-27). Since then, about 25 different kisses have been mentioned in the Bible, with the word kiss, in its various forms, occurring 46 times. However, the different kisses mentioned in the Bible had different motives behind them.

There was Jacob's kiss of affection to woo his future wife Rachael (Genesis 29:11); Joseph's kiss of forgiveness to welcome his traitorous brothers (Genesis 45:15); the murderous kiss of Joab to murder David's new army commander Amasa (2 Samuel 20:9); Absalom's kiss of flattering to steal the hearts of his father's subjects (2 Samuel 15:5); the treacherous kiss of Judas Iscariot to betray Jesus Christ (Luke 22:48); and many other kisses.

Was Orpah's kiss a kiss of affection, a kiss of betrayal, or a kiss of flattering? There is no doubt, that it was a kiss of affection. But while Orpah offered Naomi a kiss of love and affection, Ruth offered Naomi a cling of inseparable attachment. Kissing is an expression of love while, clinging to, is an expression of the heart. 'Cling to' means 'cleaving, uniting, or holding fast. By that act of clinging to, and by her famous "where you go, I will go" declaration, Ruth had dissolved her identity into that of Naomi, fully surrendering all aspects of her life into her care, willing to lay down her future to care for her.

CHAPTER THREE

Familiar Path Versus Unfamiliar Faith of Faith

For their journey of life, the two young Moabite widows were offered two diverging paths to travel on. They were to travel on either the familiar path, overtly clothed in sight, or the unfamiliar path, covertly enrobed in faith. Orpah chose the visible, familiar path, she had always been traveling on, while Ruth opted for the invisible, faith-navigated-unfamiliar path, she had never traveled on before. Both of them were driven by different circumstances for the choices they had made.

It must, however, be pointed out that familiar and unfamiliar paths are not always roads or routes or paths leading from one geographical location to another. No. Familiar and unfamiliar paths could be ideas, norms, technologies, careers, lifestyles, or ways of doing things. When you deviate from the conventional way of doing something, you are treading an unfamiliar path. The opposite is the case, when you stick to the conventional way of doing a thing, you are treading the familiar path.

The two distinct paths have their distinct natures, forms, characters, and destinations. Travelers on these two distinct paths, always have distinct motivations that actuate them to travel on the path of their choice. For Orpah and Ruth, behavioral differences played a key role in deciding their divergent preferred paths. Originally, both ladies opted for the unfamiliar path, pledging passionately to follow their mother-in-law to her hometown.

"We will go back with you to your people," they impressed upon their mother-in-law, in a language of love-driven defiance (Ruth 1:10).

However, after persistent appeals from the mother-in-law, urging them to go back to their families, and not follow her, one of them, Orpah gave in, and immediately left the unfamiliar path to tread the familiar path. But Ruth ignored the incessant pleas of the mother-in-law and continued the journey with her on the unfamiliar path.

The ease, with which Orpah gave in, to the urgings, and pleas of Naomi, as opposed to the resistance of Ruth, to the same urgings and pleas of Naomi, sums up the character trait differences between the two Moabite ladies. For Orpah, it appears she lacked that 'extra commitment' that separates success from failure. That 'extra commitment' is the passion, perseverance, and endurance usually invested in dreams to turn them into reality. Ruth, on the other hand, appears to possess the 'extra commitment' to carry on, and carry through, to realize her dream of following Naomi to Bethlehem, even at the peril of her life. Ruth had the passion, perseverance, and endurance to say, 'Until the bones are rotten', she would push on, and pull through, to give light to her dream.

On our exploratory journey through life, we need to employ the services of that 'extra commitment' of passion, perseverance, and endurance to drive home our dreams. In the absence of this, we will continuously go the Orpah way. We will leave in the middle of the road;

we will never complete our journey; we won't get to our destinations; we will not carry through our dreams.

Furthermore, Orpah could not resist the temptations of discouragement, distraction, and dissuasion, and suddenly fell to their invitations. Orpah easily gave in to the persuasions of Naomi, while Ruth was unbending, and stuck to her goal of realizing her "Where you go, I will go" declaration. Ruth never doubted in the dark, what faith told her in the light.

On our journey of life, we will certainly meet the mountains and valleys of discouragement, distraction, and dissuasion. We should, however, not allow their frightening heights and deifying depths, to intimidate us, discourage us, distract us, dissuade us, and deter us from pursuing our dreams. We should hold on fast to faith, and carry on, and carry through, to realize our dreams.

I wish to illustrate, this sort of defeatist influence, of discouragement and distraction on human progress, with an interesting story, of an American inventor called Walter Hunt. He had many inventions and patents to his name: a knife sharpener, the rope-making machine, a heating stove, a wood saw, a flexible spring, nail-making machines, inkwells, a fountain pen, a bottle stopper, firearms, and a safety pin. But his greatest invention was the sewing machine, which he designed and made in 1834. However, he tragically failed to patent it because, he was told the sewing machine would put hundreds of thousands of people engaged in hand-stitching, out of work.

A decade and two years on, the sewing machine was patented, showily carrying the name of another person, Elias Howe Jr., who began receiving royalties for the machine. Hunt launched an unsuccessful battle to reclaim his invention, but it was too late. Hunt submitted his application for a patent in 1853, seven long years after Howe had submitted his application in 1946.

Hunt paid the price for the inability to ward off discouragement, distraction, and dissuasion. You too can pay a price like this, even dearer. As you crisscross the corridors of time in your journey of life, you have to stand firm in your convictions, and not allow fear, discouragement, distraction, and dissuasion to unarm you and disarm you.

Additionally, you have to embrace the virtues of determination, passion, and endurance, and live them. These three merits are indispensable kits in the toolbox of living. Constantly deploy them. They will enable you to disable all progress-cutting leanings and help you accelerate your personal development.

Another credit point that Ruth scored, to soar up her faith to pursue her future dreams, was to dump the sorrows of her past into the litterbin of memory. She walked away from her family and her gods. Orpah, on the other hand, held on to her past and walked into her family and her gods.

We all have our gods. Our gods are anything and everything that distract us from achieving our set goals: our habits, our friends, our relations, our work, our hobbies, our places of abode, our mindsets, our culture, our marriage life, and our many things that hinder our advancement in life. Like Ruth, we should ride on faith, and walk away from them. It is the surest compass to navigate us out of our wilderness, onto our promised land. Like Ruth, we have our pasts to dump. We have pasts, beautifully wrapped up in failures, and colorfully labeled in regrets. We have to dump them into the oblivion of recall. We should not allow the regrets of the past, to steal away the greatness installed in our future. We have to bury the past in the past and look up to the future as our lifeline.

As Apostle Paul succinctly puts it, "Brothers and sisters, I do not consider myself yet to have taken hold of it. But one thing I do: Forgetting what is behind and straining towards what is ahead, I press on toward the goal to win the prize for which God has called me heavenward in Christ Jesus" (Philippians 3:13-14).

Yes, ahead of us all, is a fulfilling future. We have to strain to fully own it, and use it, to win the coveted trophy of success, in the marathon race of life. However, we can only do this, when we write an obituary for our past and never allow it to haunt and undermine our progress.

Undeniably, we all walk the paths of Orpah and Ruth in our daily walk. We are either an ***Orpahian*** or a ***Ruthenian***. Whether in business or commerce, politics or religion, academia or entertainment, or anything that promotes human subsistence, we display either ***Orpahian*** or ***Ruthenian*** disposition. We either ride on the familiar path of Orpah or the unfamiliar path of Ruth. Our motivations determine the path we take. Though the two paths lead us to different destinations, they have two things in common. They all have their motivations and their consequences.

While the unfamiliar path of faith looks risky and leads to unfamiliar territory, it has a promising future. The familiar path, on the other hand, is predictive, appears reassuring, and leads to familiar territory, but it invariably ends in a gloomy future.

The familiar path shepherded Orpah to her familiar territory of Moab, where she met her family members and friends, and together they enjoyed the familiar Moabite culture. However, she ended up as only a footnote to the bigger story choreographed by her comrade-in-widowhood, Ruth.

In contrast, the unfamiliar path of faith took Ruth to the unfamiliar territory of Bethlehem, where she manifested the glory of God, but at a cost. He lost sight of her nation, family, friends, and culture. She endured hardships, ridicule, and near rejection in her new abode, forcing her to become a farm hand, engaged in a near-beggary job, to enable her to secure her survival and that of her esteemed mother-in-law. But in the end, the glory of God sent her to the zenith of fame, crowning her a foremother of the Messiah, Jesus Christ.

And Ruth was not alone in treading the unfamiliar path. Several men of God of biblical times did so. Noah treaded the unfamiliar path, sailing in unfamiliar waters, in an unfamiliar vessel, carrying unfamiliar passengers, to an unfamiliar destination. Abraham responded to an unfamiliar call of God, packed bags and packages, trod the unfamiliar path with his family, on an 8,000-kilometre-journey, to relocate to an unfamiliar land, met unfamiliar people and events, encountered unfamiliar problems, and was in the end, decorated with the unfamiliar "Father of all Nations" title.

Joseph treaded the unfamiliar path as he was sold into slavery in unfamiliar Egypt, living in an unfamiliar home, dumped in an unfamiliar prison, and eventually elevated to an unfamiliar commanding seat of power. Moses treaded the unfamiliar path, obeying an unfamiliar call of God, and embarked on an unfamiliar journey with his compatriots, through an unfamiliar wilderness, heading to an unfamiliar promised land. Saul-turned-Paul treaded the unfamiliar path, sailing in unfamiliar waters, crisscrossing unfamiliar borders, exposed to unfamiliar shipwrecks, unfamiliar snake bites, unfamiliar flogging, unfamiliar stoning, and unfamiliar imprisonment, to emerge the author of half of the books of the New Testament of the Bible and planter of churches.

Indeed, the unfamiliar path has always been familiar to people who allow their lives to be faithfully directed by faith. These men of God took the risk, to travel on the unfamiliar path to unknown destinations, to actualize the promises of God. In reality, unfamiliar path travelers are risk-takers. They have a sense of adventure and are always ready to embrace change, to sample new environments and their constituents.

Noah undertook a sailing adventure, in the flooding waters to a world, he did not know, to actualize God's promise of judgment and salvation for the sinful and the righteous. Abraham undertook a relocation adventure into the unknown wilderness, to actualize God's promise of making him great. Joseph undertook a forced adventure into Egypt, to actualize God's promise of blessing all the families of the earth through Abraham. Moses led migrating Israelites to undertake a relocation adventure into the unknown wilderness, to actualize God's promise of giving a promised land to his chosen nation. Ruth undertook a relocation adventure into a world she did not know, to actualize the divine plan for the birth of Christ the Messiah.

You are also a qualified candidate to be used, to actualize the promise of God because you were made in the image of God, just like the biblical Abrahams, Noahs, Ruths, Esthers, and many others, who made themselves available, as vessels for making good, the plans and promises of God for the human race.

Like all adventurers, unfamiliar path travelers of the Old Testament times were bold, and their boldness was expressed in *action verbs*. Noah **built** the ark; Abraham **left** his home; Ruth **followed** Naomi; Abel **offered** a superior sacrifice; Isaac **blessed** his sons; Jacob **blessed** Joseph's children. Moses **lifted** the rod over the Red Sea and divided it; the Israelites **marched** around the city, while the priests **blew** their horns, and the walls of Jericho fell.

Moses *raised* his hand, and Israel was winning the battle against the Amalekites and ultimately won. The priests bearing the ark *dipped* their feet into the flooded waters of the Jordan River, and the river parted, paving the way for the people to pass over to the opposite side. Joshua *raised* his arm, urging God to halt the sun's movement and give his forces more time to fight by daylight, and God stopped the sun, and also unleashed a storm of hail and fire, helping Israel to defeat the enemy. David *took* a stone from his bag, *slung* it, and struck Goliath in the forehead, and he fell on his face to the ground.

Action words: **build, bless, leave, dip, follow, offer, raise, march, blow, take, sling**. These were the powerful words, deployed to the spiritual warfare battlefields, by unfamiliar path voyagers of biblical times, to turn looming defeats into victories. You, too, can deploy these action-loaded words into action, to turn your seeming impossible, possible. But you have to deploy your action words, with faith, and by faith, because these words can only produce miracles, if and when, they are fortified by faith.

Surprisingly, unfamiliar path travelers used by God to actualize His plans and promises are not angels; they are not always perfect. As offspring of Edenic Adam, they fell short of the glory of God. Noah was a drunkard. Abraham, the friend of God, was a liar; he lied about his wife. Isaac, the son of Abraham, was also a liar; he too, lied about his wife. Jacob, Isaac's son was a conman; he lived the life of a manipulator and a deceiver.

Joseph, Jacob's beloved son, was an insensitive braggart, boasting of dreams elevating him to higher heights. Moses was a murderer, and a quick-tempered leader who, in anger, struck the rock, instead of speaking to it, as God had instructed. David was an adulterer; Solomon was a womanizer; Gideon was a doubter. The Moses-led migrating Israelites were a sorrowful consignment of ungrateful complainers.

Peter was overconfident, and overconfidence blinded him to deny and betray his best friend and master Jesus three times. Jonah abdicated duty; Paul, the planter of churches, was a persecutor of the Church, killing and torturing followers of Christ. Mary Magdalene, the first person in the universe to see the risen Christ, was possessed by seven demons. Zacchaeus, the taxman, who treaded the unfamiliar path of climbing a sycamore tree to see Jesus and listen to his teaching, was very short in stature but very tall in corruption.

However, despite their pitfalls, they all invariably submitted to the will of God, and ably fitted into God's plan for the redemption of humanity. Notwithstanding your pitfalls, you too can fit into God's plan for the salvation of the human race, if you submissively submit to the will of God.

Even the failures of these unfamiliar path travelers inspired the world. David always acknowledged his sins and profusely displayed acts of repentance. He demonstrated the power of repentance to the world. Acclaimed as the wisest person in the world, Solomon had his pitfall in womanizing, having 700 wives and 300 concubines, pointing out the stark fact that wisdom alone, cannot prevent us from falling prey to vanity. The virtue of wisdom has to seek the presence of God, to win all races, including the race against vanity.

Unlike Judas Iscariot, Peter confessed as soon as he realized he had betrayed Jesus, stuck to the faith, and became the head of the Church of Christ, drumming home the message of confession and the accompanying forgiveness. Saul, a notorious persecutor of the Church, became Apostle Paul, a foremost planter of churches, telling us that the door is wide open for all, everyone and anyone, to receive Jesus, and expand the kingdom of God. Even, today's notorious murderers and armed robbers can become acclaimed pastors and bishops tomorrow. Jesus is always on duty receiving everyone and anyone who calls on him, every time, anytime, anywhere.

In the election of people to actualize His plans, God has always been very democratic. He picks people from all walks of life and in all challenges of life. In the holy line-up of people, God had used in the Bible times, to actualize His plans, were men and women of varying callings and varying characters. In the pious parade, could be found the **Drunkard** Noah, the **Liar** Abraham, the **Liar** Isaac, the **Conman** Jacob, the **Braggart** Joseph, the **Temperamental** Moses, the **Escapist** Jonah, and the **Adopted Orphan** Esther.

There were likewise the **Quitter** Peter, the **Widow** Ruth, the **Immoral** David, and the **Womanizer** Solomon. Also, the line-up, was the **Prostitute** Rahab, the **Persecutor** Paul, the **Demon-Possessed** Mary Magdalene, the

Physician Luke, the **Corrupt Taxman** Zacchaeus, the **Deserter** Demas, the **Rebel** Onesimus, and the **Servant** Tychicus.

However, all these men and women with questionable characters, had something unquestionable that endeared God, to use them. Noah was extremely patient, spending 120 years building the ark and preaching repentance. Abraham was a man of exceeding faith and was undoubtedly, called "Father of Faith. Isaac was obedient, patient, and a peacemaker, who had faith in God. Jacob was a man of faith. Joseph was a man of character, faith, integrity, humility, and discipline, who chose godly fear over sin. Moses was overwhelmingly humble, the humblest human being the world has ever seen.

David was a man after God's own heart. He had faith and trust in God, exuded love, obedience, repentance, humility, integrity, and forgiveness, and was always worshipping God. Solomon was a humble and obedient man, committed to fairness and justice, who was rewarded with a gift of wisdom, making him the wisest man of all time. Peter was a teachable, committed, and repentant disciple who put God first. Paul was spirit-led, humble, fearless, compassionate, faithful, honest, and adjudged to be someone possessing a servant's heart.

Ruth was loyal, humble, kind, hardworking, generous, and faithful. Esther was a woman of great patience, humility, obedience, wisdom, faith, and caring. Rahab had faith in God and acted on it, as and when she needed, to do so. Through her warm interaction with Joshua's two spies, Rahab exhibited a high degree of hospitality, faith, mercy, patience, and repentance.

Mary Magdalene was energetic and full of faith, gratitude, and generosity. She was so generous that she committed her resources to helping cater to the needs of Jesus and his disciples. She was faithful and grateful to Jesus, following him to his crucifixion, and even to his tomb. Mary Magdalene, thus, became the first person in the universe, to see the risen Christ and the first to share the good news of Jesus' resurrection. Some commentators of the Bible, even, say Mary Magdalene was the first evangelist in the Christian world, as well as the first, along with other women, to give the first sermon, in the history of the church.

You, too, can develop unquestionable character traits for God to elect you, to tread the unfamiliar path of faith to actualize His plans and promises for humanity. There are, however, three rare virtues, you direly need to acquire and practice, to be a qualified candidate for God to use to honor His plans and promises. You have to be faithful, teachable, and available because all the biblical men and women, God used to make good His plans, possessed these three sterling qualities. They were all, faithful, teachable, and available.

So, remain steadfast and committed to God and His teachings, demonstrating your loyalty and trust in His promises, amid all challenges. Develop a lifelong learning mindset, opening up yourself to learn the word of God from any true man of God, anytime, anywhere, under any circumstance. Finally, be willing to submit your time, talents, and all resources to God, anytime, anywhere, under any circumstance.

While travelers on the unfamiliar path, are risk-takers and adventurous, those traveling on the familiar path are unadventurous. They are timid, cowardly, chicken-hearted, unimaginative, narrow-minded, conservative, stay-at-home, uncreative, and stay-in-the-mud. They fear failure, and always remain stuck in the mud of retrogression, thus, immobilizing advancement in life.

They are comfortable with familiarity, and always want to live in a world of familiarity: seeing the same people; making the same thing; using the same methods; encountering the same problems; proposing the same solutions; getting the same results, and living the same way. Indeed, familiar path travelers are neophobic and misogynistic. They fear change, hate change, and are unchanging.

However, familiarity has its problems, notable among which, is its ability to deflate your faith and prevent miracles from coming your way. Our Lord Jesus Christ, himself, was a classic illustration of the ability of familiarity to collapse faith and lock up miracles. Bubbling with miracles of unbelievable dimensions - restoring sight, driving away demons, making the lame walk, performing incredible healings, talking to the wind to stop, walking on water, and even resurrecting the dead - familiarity could not allow Jesus to perform miracles in his hometown, Nazareth.

In Nazareth, he was seen as the familiar Jesus, the son of the familiar carpenter and the familiar Mary; the familiar Jesus, the brother of the familiar James, the familiar Joses, the familiar Jude, and the familiar Simon; and the familiar Jesus who lived in that familiar house near that familiar spot. Familiarity stole faith from Jesus' townsmen and women and restricted Jesus from performing miracles. Indeed, without faith, the power of God cannot be called to duty. And so, the miracles refused to flow in Nazareth. This is what the familiarity path does to its travelers, completely deflating their faith and preventing them from witnessing the supernatural work of God.

Here is another interesting contest of familiarity versus unfamiliarity. It features Naaman, a renowned five-star general, commanding the Syrian army. Naaman had leprosy and was expecting Prophet Elisha to cleanse him of the disease, through the familiar healing path, of calling on the name of the Lord and waving the hand over the spot of leprosy. But when the prophet prescribed an unfamiliar healing path for him, Naaman angrily doubted it and nearly missed out on his healing. Naaman, however, had his healing, when he obediently treaded the prescribed, unfamiliar path of healing, dipping himself seven times in the Jordan River.

You see how the unfamiliar path fortified with faith, gloriously triumphed over the faith-devoid familiar path. Accessorized with faith, the unfamiliar path will triumph in all circumstances.

CHAPTER FOUR

Unfamiliar Path Finds the Glory of God

The unfamiliar path of faith opens the window to manifesting the glory of God. Steering your life, along the faith-asphalted unfamiliar path, will, undoubtedly, make you showcase the worth, the magnificence, the loveliness, and the grandeur of God's perfections, to the world. The glory of God is the aggregation of the biggest, the longest, the heaviest, the finest, the grandest, and the most wonderful things condensed in the character of God. And it is the manifestation of the presence of God, and is available to every believer, everywhere, every time, and anytime, anywhere.

However, you manifest the glory of God, at a cost. You give away something dear to you, and in return, you get the opportunity to manifest the glory of God. Saintly men and women of the Bible treaded the unfamiliar path of faith, and revealed the glory of God, at the expense of losing cherished and prized possessions. Abraham unveiled the glory of God at the cost of his home. Moses divulged the glory of God at the cost of his friends. Mary, the mother of Jesus manifested the glory of God at the cost of her reputation. Joseph transmitted the glory of God at the cost of his freedom.

It cost David many years of fighting and hiding in a cave, to exhibit the glory of God. It cost Job his family, friends, and possessions to make known the glory of God. It cost Peter his fishing livelihood, to advertise the glory of God.

It cost Jonah his prejudices and prejudgments, to display the glory of God. It cost Apostle Paul his safety, to showcase the glory of God. As Paul puts it in 1 Corinthians 10:31, ".... God's glory will demand something precious of each of us."

For Ruth, God's glory demanded the loss of her husband, the loss of her home, the loss of her nationality, and the loss of her religion, as well as the departure from her homeland to face hardships, ridicule, and near rejection. Ruth rode on the unfamiliar path to honor these demands. Faith was her propeller. Faith had for ages, been the propeller of men and women to the summit of human edification. From Noah to Abraham, Moses to David, Samuel to Elijah, Sarah to Rahab, and Elizabeth to Mary, godly personalities of the Bible drove on the unfamiliar path of faith, to turn looming disappointments into thrilling appointments.

From the disappointments of famine, fear, danger, and delay, Abraham received the appointment as the father of all nations. From the disappointment of being sold into slavery and imprisoned, Joseph received the appointment as the Prime Minister of Egypt, the No.2 man of the greatest nation on earth at the time. From the disappointment of being ridiculed as an unmarried mom-to-be, Mary received the appointment as the mother of the Messiah, Jesus Christ.

From the disappointments of being an asylum seeker at birth, in a basket, a stammerer, and a fugitive, haunted by obstacles, nuisances, betrayal, and loss of loved ones, Moses received the unique appointment to lead God's chosen nation out of slavery into freedom. He accepted the appointment, parted the waters of the Red Sea, had one-on-ones with God, received the Ten Commandments, and became the hero of the Torah, the first five books of the Old Testament of the Bible.

The Bible testifies of him saying, "Since then, no prophet has risen in Israel like Moses, whom the Lord knew face to face" (Deuteronomy 34:10). And the Lord Himself testified of him as "being very humble, and humbler than anyone else on the face of the earth" (Numbers 12:3). Moses got the unprecedented testimony from God due to his steadfast faith in the Lord.

Moses was not alone in the unparalleled demonstration of unsullied faith in the Lord. The eleventh chapter of the book of Hebrews of the New Testament created a sort of hall of faith for Jewish men and women, who rode on the wings of faith, to bring great feats to their nation and humanity at large. In chronological order, the outstanding Jewish adherents of faith in the Old Testament were inducted into the hall of faith with accompanying citations:

Abel: He was the second son of Adam and Eve, the first shepherd, and the first martyr in the Bible. He was the first to be inducted into the Hall of Faith. And the citation accompanying his induction, spoke of him saying, "By faith, Abel brought God a better offering than Cain did. By faith, he was commended as righteous when God spoke well of his offerings. And by faith, Abel still speaks, even though he is dead" (Hebrews 11:4).

It is significant to note that the difference in the sacrifices offered by Cain and Abel, was not in the fruit and sheep they offered respectively. The difference was rather in the motives behind the offerings. While Abel gave the sacrifice by faith, Cain did so without faith. Abel presented his best to God in faith that God "exists and that He rewards those who seek him" (Hebrews 11:16). Abel's faith-fueled offering was pleasing to God, while Cain's faith-void offering was not pleasing to God. Abel seasoned his offering with faith, while Cain seasoned his with doubt. However, the aroma of faith is always pleasing to God.

Enoch: He was a man who so diligently walked with God and so pleased God, that God spared him the agony of death. His induction citation in Hebrews 11:5-6 noted that it was by faith that Enoch was taken to heaven without dying. The citation also described Enoch as someone who pleased God, saying, "It is impossible to please God without faith".

Noah: He was a righteous and obedient man, and the citation given to him in Hebrews 11:7 hailed the steadfast faith he had in God, heeding the call of God, to take on seemingly unreachable and unachievable assignments. "By faith Noah, when warned about things not yet seen, in holy fear built an ark to save his family. By his faith, he condemned the world and became heir of the righteousness that is in keeping with faith." Noah was warned of the destruction of the world, an event that had not humanly occurred before. He was told to undertake the laborious task of preparing an ark and filling it with a pair of all animals in the world. He was furthermore, instructed to preach and condemn the world. Noah faithfully performed all these outwardly, impossible assignments. It takes a real depth of faith to believe and spend 120 long years to carry out these odd-seeming assignments.

Abraham: A biblical heavyweight of a personality, considered the father of faith and the father of the Jewish nation, Abraham had the longest citations. It acknowledged different areas of his faithfulness: from his faith-propelled-obedience to the call of God, to step out of his native land; through his sojourning life of faith in a foreign land; to his faith in the ability of God to keep His promises (Hebrews 11:8-19). However, the high point of his faith was his willingness to obey God's command to sacrifice his only son, Isaac, even though he knew the death of Isaac would have contradicted every promise of God. Drowned in a pool of unwavering faith, Abraham was actually in the process of slaying his son for sacrifice when God intervened and provided the needed ram for the sacrifice. This is the most amazing act of faith in the entire Bible.

Sarah: Wife of Abraham, and one of the two women inducted into the hall of faith, Sarah is considered the mother of the Jewish nation. Her citation in Hebrew 11:11 applauded her patience and a long wait, to give birth at the ripe age of 90 years, saying, "It was by faith that even Sarah was able to have a child, though she was barren and was too old. She believed that God would keep His promise."

Isaac: He was the miracle child of unyoung Abraham and Sarah, and his citation in Hebrews 11:20 says, "It was by faith that Isaac promised blessing for his future to his son, Jacob, and Esau."

Jacob: He fathered twelve sons through whom Israel got its twelve tribes. Beginning life, lying and conning, Jacob had an all-night wrestling contest with God, at the end of which, he had his hip broken and his name changed to Israel, meaning "one who prevails with God" or "he struggles with God". The citation in Hebrew 11:21, accompanying his induction says, "It was by faith that Jacob when he was old and dying, blessed each of Joseph's sons and bowed in worship as he leaned on his staff."

Joseph: A dreamer and interpreter of dreams, Joseph surrendered his entire life in obedience to God. In Hebrews 11:22, it was testified of him that, "It was by faith that Joseph when he was about to die, said confidently that the people of Israel would leave Israel. He even commanded them to take his bones with them when they left."

Moses: A towering figure in Jewish history, through whom God delivered the Ten Commandments to the nation of Israel, Moses received a powerful citation (Hebrews 11: 23-29). Though overwhelmed by weaknesses and mistakes, Moses displayed heroic faith, delivering his people from bondage in Egypt and journeying with them through the wilderness en route to the Promised Land, amid want, murmurings, and disobedience of the people.

Joshua: Strong faith and obedience to God, made it possible for Joshua to lead Israel to prevail in the battle of Jericho and finally, make it to the Promised Land. He was a faithful follower and a successful leader. Hebrews 11:30 credited him for providing the needed faith and leadership for the Israelites to enter the Promised Land, noting that, "It is by faith that the people of Israel marched around Jericho for seven days and the walls came crashing down."

Others: Many others, including Rahab, a prostitute, who by faith, became a spy for Israel, and played a major role in the fall of Jericho, were inducted into the hall of faith. Also, on the hall of faith roll call, were Gideon, one of the 12 judges of Israel; Barak, the obedient warrior; and Sampson, the judge with superhuman might but acute weaknesses of the flesh. So too, were Jephthah, the warrior and the judge; King David, the man after God's own heart; and Samuel, the prophet and the last judge of Israel.

The Bible is also brimming with near-impossible events associated with faith-intoxicated men and women. Through faith, Daniel, David, and Benaiah were able to immobilize the mouths of lions. Faith shepherded three Jewish youngsters – Shadrach, Meshach, and Abednego – to quench the ferocity of the fire. Faith boosted some too, to evade the vicious power of the sword. David escaped the swords of Goliath and Saul; Moses escaped the sword of Pharaoh; while Elijah escaped the sword of Jezebel. By faith, Jewish leaders like Joshua, David, Asa,

Jehoshaphat, Hezekiah, and Josiah were able to subdue powerful nations.

We all know the definition of faith as "the substance of things hoped for, the evidence of things not seen." Yes, faith is the spiritual equivalent of physical eyesight. Faith sees; it sees the invisible order. While the human eye sees the visible, physical world, human faith sees the invisible, spiritual world. Our physical eye sees evidence of the material world, while our faith sees evidence of the spiritual world.

Faith becomes redundant when, what we are hoping for, is there for us to see or touch. But faith is called to duty when, what we are hoping for, cannot be seen or touched. However, faith is not a mere belief nor an intellectual know-how. It is the willingness, readiness, and eagerness to trust in God, to rely on God, and to cling to God. Faith urges you to trust in God; faith drives you to rely on God; faith constrains you to cling to God, every moment and every hour of your life, through His only begotten son Jesus Christ. Faith converts impossibilities into possibilities to midwife the birth of testimonies to comfort, encourage, and edify others.

And if today, there is to be a hall of faith for people who rode on faith to turn their disappointments into appointments, will you be inducted into this hall? We all have disappointments in life. And like the great men and women of the Bible, we can also tread the unfamiliar path of faith, to convert our mournful disappointments into joyous appointments. However, like the men and women of biblical times, we too must give away something dear to us, to manifest God's glory, and convert our woeful disappointments into delightful appointments, for all to see.

And what do you want to forgo to manifest the glory of God? Is it your glory, your money, your possessions, your job, your education, your family, your friends, your sanity, or your lifestyle? You have to be ready to forgo, your anything and your everything, your all-in-all. You have to be ready to pull apart any and every obstacle, that stands between you and God. You have to be ready to go through every adversity, that puts your faith on trial and prepares you, for the great appointment God has for you, just as Joseph, the dreamer and interpreter of dreams, did.

CHAPTER FIVE

Familiar Path Breeds Grasshopper Mentality

There seems to be a 'fear virus' that infects travelers on the faith-void familiar path. This virus psychologically disables familiar-path voyagers, rendering them timid, fearful, under-resourced, and self-pitying. This make-believe virus, which has come to be known as the **grasshopper mentality**, deflates the confidence of familiar path travelers and makes them perceive themselves as heavily overwhelmed by problems, that do not, even, exist. It makes them see themselves as nothingness with no capacity to fight anything and everything, and accordingly, behave like that.

And at the sight of the slightest challenge, they recoil into their shells and seek asylum in a cannot-do mentality. They then, take up an unstable lifestyle like the orangutan, the great ape, native to rainforests of Malaysia and Indonesia, that unbelievably, relocates to a new home every day. They, subsequently, begin asking questions, murmuring, complaining, and rebelling like ungrateful migrating Israelites, wandering in the wilderness. They see themselves as limited in everything and all things. This is the fear-driven, timid-laced, defeatist mindset of people with the grasshopper mentality.

But do you know that our limitations are self-inflicted? Yes, they are. We often pick up unrealistic fears, unreasonable insecurities, and unsubstantiated negatives and allow them to undermine our self-confidence. We tend to define ourselves by our problems, not by the possibilities God has installed in us. Fear always drives us to locate our bearings on our problem chart, rather than locating them on our possibility chart.

But this should not be the case. As believers, we can do all things through Christ who strengthens us (Philippians 4:13). God has promised us all things and everything, to make life worth living for us because we are his heirs and co-heirs with Christ (Romans 8:16-17). But are we even aware of this great inheritance, and do we know how to claim and possess it?

How would you describe a man, who was given an inheritance of one trillion US dollars, but took 40 years to get to the bank to sign the necessary documents to claim the money, and begin spending it? Is it over-excitement or disbelief? This was exactly what happened to the Israelites of the Old Testament times. God gave them the inheritance of Canaan, assuring them that He would send an angel before them and drive out the Canaanites, Amorites, Hittites, Perizzites, Hivites, and Jebusites. (Exodus 33:2).

However, faithlessness traumatized them to take 40 years to claim and possess the land. They were terrorized by fear and tyrannized by disobedience to take 40 long years to make a journey of 613 kilometers from Egypt to Canaan. This is a distance, walking 18 kilometers a day, will take only 40 days to cover.

Covering a 613-kilometer distance in 40 years implies that on average, the migrating Israelites were walking just 43 meters a day. This 43-meter distance, which the migrating Israelites were traveling daily, could be covered by 23-year-old American female athlete, Sha'Carri Richardson, the 2023 World Athletics Championships 100-meter gold medalist, in just about five seconds. As for the world-renowned Jamaican sprinter, Usain Bolt, he could do it, in less than five seconds!

While the migrating Israelites were approaching the frontiers of the Promised Land after a two-year journey from Egypt, their leader Moses, responding to a directive from God, sent 12 chieftains of the 12 tribes of Israel to Canaan, to conduct reconnaissance on the land and its people. After spending 40 days on a spy mission, the twelve spies returned to submit their findings. Before Moses, Aaron, and the entire Israelite nation, the scouting team presented two reports: a majority report authored by ten spies, and a minority report endorsed by two spies.

Brandishing a cluster of grapes from the mission area, which was so large that it took two men to carry, both the majority and minority reports testified to the fertility of the land and confirmed it to be indeed, a terrain flowing with milk and honey. However, the two reports disagreed on the ability of Israel to fight and overrun the inhabitants of the land.

The majority report of ten spies identified the people of Canaan to be descendants of the renowned giant, Anak, and were as gigantic as their forebear, and were living in fortified cities. The ten spies went on, to compare their own stature to that of the Canaanites, saying, "We seemed like the grasshopper in our own eyes, and we looked the same to them." The majority report, thus, concluded that the Israelites would not be able to defeat the Canaanites. This conclusion elicited disappointments, murmurings, and rebellious actions from the Israelites, who accused Moses of pursuing a project that was undermining their very existence. They even expressed the preference for going back to Egypt to live in bondage.

In sharp contrast, the minority report authored by Joshua and Caleb acknowledged the presence of God with Israel and concluded that Israel would be able to overcome the Canaanites. Indeed, the faith-inspired minority report prevailed over the sight-inspired majority report, as the Israelites comprehensively defeated the Canaanites after seven years of war. It was a sweet victory for a minority vote of 2-10, certainly, against the principles and practice of modern democracy.

Democracy by a majority vote is good. Even the disciples of Jesus used a majority vote to democratically 'elect' Mathias as a replacement for Judas Iscariot, who had absconded after betraying Jesus. However, democracy by a majority vote is not always ideal. The majority could be made up of people infected with a grasshopper mentality as was the case of the ten spies Moses sent on the recon mission. The triumph of the majority-vote democracy in the case of the disciples, was even, preceded by prayers. The disciples sought the face of God, praying intensely before 'voting'.

There was another incredible minority-vote victory recorded in the Bible. It was an unbelievable 1-400 minority victory, chalked by a prophet called Micaiah. Against a unanimous prophecy of 400 fellow prophets,

Micaiah rightly prophesied that King Ahab of Israel would be defeated and killed in Ramoth-Gilead, in a battle with Syria (1 Kings 22: 1-40). And it came to pass, as Prophet Micaiah had prophesized, that Israel was comprehensively defeated by the Syrians, and their king, Ahab was killed in Ramoth-Gilead.

The ten spies who doubted the ability of the Israelites to over-run the Canaanites were infected with the 'fear virus'; they were displaying a grasshopper mentality. The grasshopper mentality is a self-concept, an expression of your internal sense of who you are. The grasshopper mentality makes you see people, seeing you, the way you see yourself. The ten Israelite spies saw themselves as looking like grasshoppers and believed the Canaanites also saw them look like grasshoppers. And in their own words, "We seemed like grasshoppers in our own eyes, and we looked the same to them."

But why would God ask Moses to send spies to recon a land that He had repeatedly promised the Israelites? Remember, God, first, made the Promised Land promise to Abraham, and later confirmed it to Abraham's son Isaac, then to Isaac's son Jacob, and then again, to Moses. Remember too, that God had also assured the Israelites that every place they set their foot would be theirs, and that their territory would extend from the desert to Lebanon, and from the Euphrates River to the Mediterranean Sea (Deuteronomy 11:24). Why, then, should God call for the deployment of a spy mission to explore a land that He had long, given out with a title deed, which was only waiting for possession?

It is interesting to know that, the very idea of conducting reconnaissance of the Promised Land, did not originate from God. It was first mooted by the Israelites themselves. They approached Moses and expressed the desire, to send men to spy on the Promised Land, to determine its route, and the towns along the route (Deuteronomy 1:22). Moses endorsed the idea, and sought direction and guidance from God (Deuteronomy 1:23). God subsequently approved the idea, and instructed Moses to send out men to spy out the land (Numbers 13:2).

But why should the Israelites call for the scouting of a land God had over the centuries promised them? Though their very presence in the wilderness, was a testament to the fulfillment of the good number of promises, God had made to them, they still lacked faith in God. They doubted the ability of God to deliver the land to them. They doubted their ability, to fight and defeat the inhabitants of the land.

The Promised Land promise of God was not unconditional. It had a conditionality. It was conditioned on the faith of the Israelites: their trust in God and their obedience to God. Certainly, Joshua and Caleb were aware of this conditionality. That was why they stated, "If the Lord is pleased with us, then He will bring us into this land, and give it to us" (Numbers 14:8). And the Lord can only be pleased with them when and only when, they repose their faith in Him, trusting Him and obeying Him because without faith it is impossible to please God (Hebrews 11:6).

The living manual of the Christian faith, the Bible is full of promises of God. Some bible scholars have listed about 3,000 promises of God. However, in his book ***All the Promises of the Bible***, Herbert Locklear identified **7,147** promises from God to man. Among the myriad of promises, are the promise to strengthen us; take care of our needs; give us rest; answer our prayers; protect us; be with us all the time, and give us everlasting life.

The Bible is, however, an "if" guidebook for living. Many of God's promises are premised on "if". In John 15:7, for instance, Jesus promises to 'provide us whatever we ask,' but this is contingent on us 'remaining in him and his words remaining in us.' In Matthew 5:5, we are given the promise of inheriting the Earth, but this promise is dependent on us being gentle, humble, and meek.

God has attached "ifs" to His promises. We have to fulfill these conditionalities for God to make good His promises. It means we have a role to play in motivating God to fulfill His promises. In the case of the Promised Land promise of God, the Israelites were expected to play the role of reposing their faith in God, trusting Him, believing Him, and obeying Him.

God thus, used the spy mission to test the faith of the Israelites, just as He had tested Abraham's faith in Genesis 22:1, asking him to offer his son Isaac for sacrifice. God was in the business of testing people's faith in biblical times, and He is today, in the same business of testing our faith. Proverbs 17:3 says, "The crucible for silver and the furnace for gold, but the Lord tests the heart." Like the migrating Israelites, our problem is our hearts. Our hearts are hardened. And as God's promises are premised on our faith, God is constantly testing us, to know if our hearts are seeking Him or seeking the mentality of the grasshopper.

The grasshopper mentality begins with a low estimation of ourselves. The ten spies were motivated by fear to give a low estimation of themselves. They saw themselves looking as little as the grasshopper and believed the Canaanites would also see them like grasshoppers. Like Orpah, the fears of the ten Jewish spies were so large that, they doubted the sufficiency of God, the primary source of their power.

People with the grasshopper mentality, always think they are so much smaller than the opposition. They see themselves as not having the ability to overcome. They see themselves as nobodies and losers. They are doubt-casters. They begin with 'we can't' and move to exaggerate the truth. They always think "We are not good enough to do this or that." Their words and actions always reflect their way of thinking.

Practitioners of grasshopper mentality, lack faith and always limit their resources to what is available by sight. They are naysayers, and are always pessimistic, labeling every challenging situation as hopeless and hapless. They see a partially filled glass of water, and say it is half empty, instead of saying it is half full. They look at the negative side of things and ignore the positive side, even if the positive overshadows the negative. Their perception becomes their reality. They allow what is a big problem to become illogically a bigger problem. Devotees of the

grasshopper mentality, seem not to know the power of God.
- That God is all-powerful, all-knowing, all-seeing, kind, gracious, faithful, and never weary;
- That God breaks through impossible barriers to offer help in impossible situations;
- That God is always there for them, and is with them;
- That God is their refuge and strength;
- That God loves them, and His son, Jesus has conquered the world for them and has made them more than conquerors.

The opposite of the grasshopper mentality is the overcomer's mentality, conqueror's mentality, or winner's mentality. People with overcomer mentality subsist on 1 John 5:4, believing that "…. everyone born of God overcomes the world…." They invariably meditate on things that are true, noble, just, pure, lovely, and of good report (Philippians 4:8). They always tune their minds to praising God as King David, an astute overcomer continuously did (Psalm 42: 5&11).

People with the overcomer mentality are strong-willed and hardly give up on any task they set for themselves. As American Clergyman Dr. Jose G. Rodriguez points out:
- Overcomers do not settle for what happens but make things happen (Philippians 2:5).
- Overcomers see setbacks as a setup for a comeback (Isaiah 54:17).

- Overcomers do not set limitations (Philippians 4:13; Proverbs 4:23).
- Overcomers speak life amid death (Psalm 23:4).
- Overcomers want to live victorious in all circumstances (John 16:33).

Overcomers fortify themselves with Joshua 5:13-15, faithfully relying on the three things that God told Joshua on the outskirts of paganistic Jericho, while the Israelites were battle-readying for the conquer of Jericho and possession of the Promised Land:
- **I am the commander of the army of the Lord**, meaning, 'the Lord is in command, anywhere, and everywhere the believer steps.'
- **You are not alone**, meaning 'the Lord is always with the believer.'
- **You are on holy ground**, meaning 'anywhere and everywhere the believer steps, is holy ground, even if it is a demonic terrain like paganistic Jericho.'

It is important to point out here that, though, Naomi's better half, Elimelech took an overcomer's stride by treading an unfamiliar path to Moab, he was not an overcomer. Had he been an overcomer, he would have deployed to practice, attributes of the overcomer's mentality, and would not have even, made the escape journey to Moab with his family. He would have rather stayed at home and used the famine setback as a setup for a comeback for something bigger and larger, to overcome the famine.

Elimelech rather had the grasshopper mentality. He was overwhelmed with ignorance, fear, pessimism, self-pity, negativism, faithlessness, and low estimation of the physical and spiritual resources at his disposal. He lacked the winner's mentality premised on the assurance that God is always at work, making good His promises, and that He is ever ready to respond to our calls.

On the other hand, Joshua and Caleb, the two spies, who authored the positive, minority report on the reconnaissance mission to the Promised Land, exhibited the overcomer's mentality. Unlike Orpah, and like Ruth, Joshua, and Caleb had no fears and never doubted the sufficiency of God, the primary source of their power. They had the attitude of 'God says it, and it shall be done.' Joshua and Caleb derived their positive mentality from the promise of God, not from their own strength. They did not base their verdict on what they saw, but on what God had said about delivering a promised land to the Israelites.

Paul vividly summarized the mentality of Joshua and Caleb in 2 Corinthians 4:18, when he said "So we fix our eyes not on what is seen, but on what is unseen. For what is seen is temporary, but what is unseen eternal." God had promised them, the land they had not seen, but they trusted God, and fixed their eyes on it, with faith. And God delivered it to them.

Like the Israelites of the Old Testament times, we all have our promised lands flowing with niceties of good living: good health, good education, good job, good marriage,

good family, enduring prosperity, and salvation. But we have to claim and possess our individual promised lands by faith. We have to walk the walk of Joshua and Caleb, trusting and obeying God. We have to be Ruthenians, walking the walk of Ruth to access our lands, and manifest the glory of God. We can only do this when we abandon the grasshopper mentality and take up the overcomer's mentality with faith, as Joshua and Caleb did by:
- Focusing on the greatness of God
- Not being intimidated and overwhelmed by their enemies
- Not being overwhelmed and moved by their circumstances
- And focusing on what they would enjoy once they entered the Promised Land.

Whenever we find ourselves under the curse of the grasshopper mentality, we should remember that:
- We are a precious creation of God, made in the image of God;
- We are adopted children of God, ransomed through the sacrificial death of Jesus on the cross.
- Our power comes from the Holy Spirit indwelling us.
- God did not give us a spirit of fear, but a spirit of power, and love, and of self-control" (2 Timothy 1:7).

Though the Israelites were at the borders of the Promised Land, fear terrorized them to wander in the wilderness for 38 more years. While the inhabitants of Canaan were looking at the God of Israel and were shaking like a leaf, the Israelites themselves, who had on countless occasions, experienced the mighty power of God, were looking at their own strength, and not the power of God, and were intimidated into disbelief.

In our daily walk, we face spiritual battles against Satan and his collaborators, against the world and its attractions, and flesh and its enticements. While Satan and his collaborators look at our God and begin shaking like a leaf, we tend to look at our own strengths and are intimidated into unbelief and disbelief that God would not deliver us. Like the biblical Israelites, fear has terrorized us and kept us wandering in our wilderness for a long time. Fear is keeping us from entering our promised land.
To overcome the torments of fear, we have to undress the grasshopper mentality and enrobe in the overcomer's mentality with the knowledge that:
- There is nothing bigger than the Almighty God
- He is the creator, omnipotent, the sustainer
- His promises are true
- His word is infallible
- He loves us and cares for us.

The grasshopper mentality is a prison yard of inability. Your continued incarceration there, will not help you. Refrain from the low estimation of your capabilities. Stop mourning your perceived inabilities and celebrate the innumerable abilities God has installed in you. Do not allow fear to make you doubt your abilities. Take off the cannot-do mentality, you are wearing, and dress up in a can-do mentality. Do away with limited thinking. It produces limited abilities that only bring limited results.

Do not focus on only one part of a picture, and rush at a verdict. Focus on the picture in its entirety. Maybe, there are jewels and gems hidden in obscure parts of the picture, that could give you a spirit-lifting song to sing. Do not allow fear, to keep you wandering in your wilderness, and sway you away, from entering your promised land. Employ the power of faith to overcome fear.

A society's culture is derived from either a familiar path or an unfamiliar path. This determines society's way of living and defines its corporate personality and identity. An unfamiliar path creates a dynamic society in which 'change' is the currency with which all transactions are conducted. A dynamic society always engages in ceaseless change, altering, reforming, and reformatting the way of living of its people. It transforms its environment, improves its conditions of living, and recasts its worldview.

On the other hand, a familiar path creates a static society that abhors change and is happy with the status quo. People in this kind of society, are happy to live in a changeless environment. They frown on innovation, invention, and discovery. They lead a regimental life, strictly regulated by tradition. Their beliefs, as well as their social, political, business, and legal environments, are controlled by tradition. People in this kind of society, are only a prototype of their forebears. They hate experimentation and change and lack advancement in life. However, human refinement is always attained in an environment of dynamism, where experimentation, change, innovation, and competition dominate. A dynamic culture produces higher values of knowledge and mastery over nature, safety, moral refinement, comfort, and freedom.

Travelers on a familiar path, enjoy a cozy ride to familiar destinations and meet familiar problems. In contrast, travelers on an unfamiliar path, encounter rough and stormy rides to unknown destinations and meet unfamiliar problems, but feed on faith and hard work, to discover their destiny. They possess Lincolnesque dispositions of honesty, empathy, humility, perseverance, courage, intellect, vision, responsibility, civility, and leadership, which they adequately deploy with strong faith, to 'rise from mat to mattresses.'

CHAPTER SIX

The Mount Horebs on The Unfamiliar Path

There are always Horeb mountains on unfamiliar paths. These mountains function as transit points for unfamiliar-path travelers. Mount Horeb, also known as Mount Sinai or the Mountain of God, is a famed peak on the Israel-Egypt frontier, believed to, spiritually denote the presence and power of God. It was on this mountain that Moses had a life-changing encounter with God. It was on the same Mount Horeb that the Israelites sealed a renewed covenant with God, after fleeing from bondage in Egypt.

Mount Horeb was also the place, where Moses received the Ten Commandments and the laws, rules, and instructions for the fleeing Israelites, to effectively reorganize themselves, for the journey to the Promised Land. Mount Horeb, again, provided a sanctuary for the powerful Hebrew prophet, Elijah, who fled from the wrath of power-hungry, violent, and whorish Queen Jezebel, and sought asylum in a cave, on the mountain. Like Moses, Elijah spent 40 days on the mountain and had an extraordinary encounter with God.

And as you embark on the journey of life on the unfamiliar road, you will certainly, stumble upon your Mount Horeb. It will give you a life-changing experience as Moses, Elijah, and the entire on-the-journey Israelite nation had on the biblical Horeb mountain. Your Mount Horeb may not be a mountain per se. It may be your job, your place of abode, your friends, your family, your educational qualification, your hobby, or the harnessing of a fraction of your talent.

On your Horeb mountain, you will discover your comfort zone, and derive relative joy and happiness from it. You will so, be overwhelmed by the qualified joy and happiness you are enjoying on your Horeb mountain, that you will not have the urge, to forge ahead, to climb up, the ladder of progression. Your Mount Horeb could therefore be anything and everything that seems to give you relative financial security, comfort, honor, and self-satisfaction, and makes you unworried, to seek higher heights.

There are, indeed, perceived glittering gems, in the form of relative joy and happiness, on your Horeb mountain, that could daze you, to hastily conclude that, you have reached the elastic limit of your potential. But you might not have reached anywhere near your optimal. Possibly, you might have harnessed only 1% of your potential. The remaining 99% is waiting to be harnessed.

You should, therefore, not be excited and satisfied with your stay on your Mount Horeb. There, is not your destination. Your destination is your Canaan, the full 100% potential in you to be released. That is your promised land. And it is located far, beyond your Horeb mountain.

Mount Horeb is only a transit point and not a destination. It is a place to freshen up, rest, and acquire character and strength to pursue the circuitous journey to your promised land. Mount Horeb is only a temporary place to stay, to wise up. It is there, that you go through the rigorous of character-building, to up your learning curve, to acquire character, to fight on, and fight through, to attain the ultimate in life. It is a launching pad to greatness. There are many Mount Horebs on the road to life, and they are not destinations but transit points to check in and check out to continue the journey of life.

Mount Horeb was a transit point for the on-the-journey-Israelites to learn, train, build, and organize for the arduous warfare and journey to the Promised Land. At Horeb, the Israelites received a civil code for regulating their individual and communal living. At Horeb, the Israelites built the Tabernacle, a House of God, a mobile place of worship that would remind them of the presence of God, and provide them strength, direction, guidance, family delineation, and focus in their journey through the wilderness.

At Horeb, the Israelites trained a group of their countrymen and women, the Levites to prudently administer and care for the Tabernacle. At Horeb, the Israelites conducted a census to determine their population mix to organize themselves into groups for effective planning and administration. At Horeb, the Israelites formed a 603,550-man-strong military force, in preparedness for the numerous battles ahead of them, in their quest to possess the Promised Land. Horeb, thus organized Israelites into formidable political, military, social, economic, and religious units with shared responsibilities, in readiness for the spiritual and military warfare ahead of them, on their way to the Promised Land.

So it is always, with the journey of life, via the unfamiliar route. You will encounter a Mount Horeb on your way. A stay on this mountain will make life comparably homelier and cozier for you. You will be guaranteed bread and butter, a roof over your head, security, comfort, respect, and in fact, all the necessities of life. But Horeb is not your home. You do not have to stay there for far, too long. It is not your destination. You have a Canaan far beyond the Horeb mountain, to go in, to possess.

At their transit camp at the foot of the Horeb mountain, the traveling Israelites had a reasonably gratifying life. They had enough to eat and enough to drink, in a barren land. They were provided food in the form of manna from heaven, which they harvested every morning, except on the Sabbath. They had a regular supply of water flowing from a rock on Mount Horeb. They were safely secured, as they did not encounter frequent enemy attacks.

The pedestrian goodies, the Israelites were enjoying at Horeb, made them become complacent and forget their journey. They became adamant about continuing the journey and virtually made Horeb a home. They spent close to a whole year, camping there, seemingly abandoning the divine project of "going in, to possess the Promised Land." The apparent abdication of duty, prompted God to give them a wake-up call, saying:

".... You have stayed long enough at this mountain. Break camp and advance into the hill country of the Amorites; go to all the neighboring peoples in Arabah, in the mountains, in the western foothills, in the Negev and along the coast to the land of the Canaanites and to

Lebanon, as far as the great river, the Euphrates. See, I have given you this land. Go in and take possession of the land the Lord swore he would give to your fathers – to Abraham, Isaac, and Jacob – to their descendants after them" (Deuteronomy 1: 6-8 NIV).

The Lord was urging the traveling Israelites to break camp and check out from Horeb, to check in at their intended destination, Canaan. Indeed, it was God who created Mount Horeb, and He, alone, knew the purpose, for which the mountain was created. The mountain might have been created to function as a transit point, and only a transit point, alone, not a home. That was why God gave a similar wake-up call to Prophet Elijah, a fugitive, fleeing from the rage of Queen Jezebel, who sought asylum in a cave on Mount Horeb. God called Elijah and twice, asked him, "What are you doing here?"

With the "What are you doing here?" query, God was rebuking Elijah for abdicating his prophetic duty with his continuous stay on the mountain. The Lord, accordingly, ordered him to check out of the mountain and check into his base, to perform prophetic duties of anointing a king in Syria and Israel, as well as anointing Elisha to assist him. Mount Horeb has never been a home, and will never be a home. It has always been a transit point for acquiring character and strength for propelling to the highest point of attainment.

Life is all, about progression; moving from one level of progress to the next level of progress; checking out from a lower level of progression, and checking in to a higher level of progression. A fulfilling life frowns on stagnation. It yearns for progression, relocating from the good to the better, and the better to the best. It aims at the summit, the ultimate, the yummiest, and nothing else.

It was for the attainment of the ultimate for his compatriots, that Moses had for over 40 times, urged his countrymen and women to break camp at Horeb and "go in and possess the land" God had promised them. The Mount Horebs, we encounter at the various junctions of life, offer us the opportunity to learn, train, build, and organize ourselves, in readiness, to check out and check in to possess our Canaan.

There are always obstacles to checking out, from the seeming comfort zone of Horeb to checking into the unfamiliar promised land of Canaan. The obstacles are mostly psychological. There are the lack-of-faith-driven obstacles of distrust and mistrust, unbelief and disbelief, disinformation, and misinformation, the lack of confidence, fear of failure, fear of the unknown, fear of change, fear of fear, and complacency of bedding with the status quo. "The old order has given me a fine home, a fine marriage, a fine car, a fine position, and indeed, a fine personality in society; why do I, then, experiment with the untested new order?"

However, the fine possessions we adore, and are very content with, on our Horeb mountain, could be only an inkling of the potential greatness installed in us. We may not have possessed all the lands willed to us in Canaan. We must therefore press on and fight on, with faith, to go in, to possess all our lands. The challenges of entering the promised land, and comprehensively possessing the lands are enormous. And this always deters us from venturing to bed with a checkout.

For the Israelites, they had to crisscross the lanes of obedience and disobedience, belief and disbelief, trust and distrust, encouragement and discouragement, faith and faithlessness; navigate the raging waters of the Jordan River; pull down the impregnable walls of Jericho; and go to war with the numerous hostile nations inhabiting the land. Even after Joshua had led them to enter the Promised Land, fighting and defeating 31 different kings, God reminded the then-90-year-old army commander that "There are still very large areas of land to possess." (Joshua 13:1).

It was the acts of faith and obedience that made it possible for the Israelites to dismantle the hurdles on their way to the Promised Land. Obedience, reinforced by faith, propelled Joshua to comply with the divine plans God had prescribed for overcoming the hurdles of crossing the flooding waters of the Jordan River and pulling down the walls of Jericho. The faith-inspired twosome triumphs were a game-changer for the Israelites. Hebrews 11:30 aptly sums it up, saying, "By faith, the walls of Jericho fell."

We all have our own lanes of obedience and disobedience, belief and disbelief, trust and distrust, encouragement and discouragement, faith and faithlessness to crisscross. We all have our own raging waters of a Jordan River to navigate. We have all our own impregnable Jericho walls to pull down. We all have our own spiritually hostile kings to fight and defeat. And as the Field-Marshal Joshua-led Israelites deployed obedience-fueled-faith to overpower the raging waters of Jordan, pull down the impenetrable walls of Jericho, and defeat the hostile kings of Canaan, we too, can deploy obedience-fertilized-faith to overcome the hurdles on our way, to possessing our promised land.

In other words, we have to travel on a faith-compassed unfamiliar road, obediently checking in and checking out at the various Mount Horebs on our way, till we reach our promised land. Checking in and checking out, have always been part of human history. The great civilizations that history has bequeathed to us, are all products of check-ins and check-outs. The super-power United States of America we know today, is a product of people checking out from their diverse Horeb mountains across the globe, to check into the American dream. The economic success story of tiny Singapore, the "Little Red Dot" which we admire today, is a product of checkouts and check-ins of people from their diverse Horeb mountains across the *Yellow Continent*.

There were many checkout points and check-in points in bible times. Haran was a checkout point for Abraham to embark on the journey into the Promised Land. Jacob had his checkout point at the Jabbok River where he wrestled with God, and had his name changed to Israel, meaning "Let God Prevail". The Prison was the checkout point for Joseph before entering Pharaoh's Palace to become a prime minister.

David had the Cave as a checkout point, from where he checked in to become the King of Israel. Paganistic Moab was the checkout point for Ruth, from where she checked into Naomi's home in Bethlehem, and eventually checked into Boaz's home to become the mother of Obed, grandmother of Jesse, and eventual foremother of Jesus Christ the Messiah.

We do not only check out from geographical locations, but we also check out from situations, habits, and vices. We check out our sinful past, our defeatist past, our alcoholism past, our nomadic past, our poverty-infested past, our miserable past, and many other pasts shrinking our progress. An organized act can also be a checkout point. Paul's organized act of persecuting followers of Christ was the checkout point for him to check in to become a zealous apostle of Christ. Paul checked out from his base in Jerusalem on his way to Damascus to persecute followers of Christ, only to have an encounter with Christ himself, and miraculously check into the vineyard of Christ.

We check out an ugly past to check into a fulfilling future. Joseph, the favorite son of Jacob, was a classic illustration of the initiation from a disappointing past to a gratifying future. He checked out a gloomy and doomy past to check into a gratifying and rewarding future. His brothers betrayed him, throwing him into a pit and subsequently, selling him into slavery. In slavery, his master's wife tried to seduce him but he refused. The refusal compelled the master's wife to frame him up as a rapist, landing him in prison. He endured a demeaning prison life, only to check out from prison to check into Pharaoh's Palace as the second in command of the then-most powerful nation in the world. He became the Prime Minister of Egypt.

When we check out the past, we shouldn't allow its devastations, pains, and feelings of bitterness of the past to cloud the rewarding future on our horizons. We shouldn't allow the ghosts of the dead past to haunt us and take us, hostage. We should instead, take the past hostage, by consigning it to the dustbin of memory. We should forgive the people who inflicted the painful past on us. Here, again, there can't be any better illustration than Joseph.

Joseph forgivingly pardoned his brothers who sold him into slavery, saying, "You intended to harm me, but God intended it for good to accomplish what is now being done, the saving of many lives" (Genesis 50:20). Joseph forgot all his past troubles, and looked forward to a fruitful future. He named his first son Manasseh, meaning "Forgotten Troubles," and the second son Ephraim, meaning "Twice Fruitful."

As we check out the mournful past and check into a reassuring future, we should stir up the talents God has deposited in us, and exercise them to keep them alive. An under-utilized talent is no better than a neglected talent. Like all things, a neglected talent depreciates, loses value, and becomes irrelevant and a deficit to the owner and society at large. We can stir up and exercise our talents only when we check out from our comfort zones at the transit points on our Horeb mountains.

Turning a transit point into a final destination is a snare, that robs us of the glittering golden crown of glory that God has in store for each of us. God does not want us to settle for bronze or silver. He has ordained each one of us, to reach out for the ultimate gold. That is why He has installed in us the immense potential for greatness. Cozying up at a transit point, harnessing only 10% of your potential, means you have not yet arrived.

You only arrive when you are in your Canaan, your final destination, harnessing the complete 100% of your potential. Leaving behind, the comfort zone of Mount Horeb, arriving in your Canaan, and making it your residence, brings with it spirit-stirring and heart-warming benefits: personal growth, increased confidence, new opportunities, new experiences, and eventual frog-leap into the world of your dreams, to dine with self-actualization. You will own a sense of accomplishment, and ride on the joy of accomplishment.

So, let's arrive. Let's harness our talents to the fullest. Let's get to the elastic limit of our potential. Mount Horeb is not a home; it is a comfort zone, a transit point. Let's split up with complacency and mediocracy, break our camps at our Horeb mountains, and hurry to our Canaan, to possess our promised lands. In Canaan, our blessings are assured, and will divinely multiply.

However, we must remember that the mathematical rules of multiplication apply in the kingdom of Canaan too. Are you aware that, in divine multiplication, you are the multiplicand? Yes, you are. You are the number that has to be multiplied, and God, is the multiplier, the number by which the multiplicand is multiplied. And God divinely multiplies what you have, by the blessings He has for you. And if today, God wants to bless you a billion or zillion times, it means He wants to multiply what you have; your wealth, your multiplicand by a billion or a zillion times. But if you have nothing, no wealth at all, and your multiplicand is zero, you can't become a billionaire or a zillionaire. You will remain poor and wealthless because zero multiplied by any number remains zero. So, it takes you and your efforts to receive God's gift of divine multiplication.

In the two miracles Jesus performed to feed a multitude of thousands of people, there were multiplicands: the five loaves of bread with two pieces of fish in possession of a young boy; and the seven loaves of bread with a few small fish the disciples had.

In both cases, Jesus asked his disciples an important question: "What do you have; How many loaves do you have?" It was the multiplicands of five loaves of bread with two pieces of fish and the seven loaves of bread with a few small fish, that Jesus used to perform the divine multiplication to feed the multitude of thousands of people, with a leftover of several baskets of loaves. What is your multiplicand? What do you have? Without a multiplicand, you can't experience the miracle of divine multiplication.

CHAPTER SEVEN

Unfamiliar Path Subsists on Hard Work

Faith becomes real when it is demonstrated in desperate situations: at the risk of losing your work, your reputation, your membership in a group, your security, and even your life. There is always an undisputable transmission of God's divine power, in response to the demonstration of real acts of faith. It could be an immediate or long time or even super-long time. No matter the time, the divine-power transmission process will certainly, take place. Faith is, therefore, the transmission line through which God transmits His supernatural power, to contain and overpower challenges, to turn the impossible, possible.

Faith, however, feeds on hard work and courage. Faith, unaccompanied by hard work and courage is a risky theory in economics, and indeed, every human discipline. An unfamiliar step of courage is always needed to turn faith into sight, to see the manifestations of the fruit of faith.

The Jewish woman bleeding profusely for twelve years, took an unfamiliar step of courage, to touch the garment of Jesus, to get a cure for her ailment. Abraham took an unfamiliar step of courage, to journey from his native home to the unfamiliar land God had promised him, before securing and practicalizing the title "Father of all Nations". Ruth took the unfamiliar step of courage, to labor in Boaz's field to win his heart and eventually, have him as a husband.

Hastings Banda of Malawi took an unfamiliar step of courage, walking 1,000 miles from his native land to South Africa, to work and study, and proceeding to the US, to study to become a doctor, only to return home, to become the first president of his country. Esther Ocloo of Ghana took an unfamiliar step of courage, to begin a marmalade business, with less than one dollar, grew it into a global inspiration to propel her, to become a co-founder of the Women's World Banking, and a recipient of the highly acclaimed Africa Prize for Leadership award.

No amount of fasting and prayer will turn your faith into sight if you do not accompany it with work. You have to, courageously step out, and take the cliff of your comfort zone. As you do this, you will begin stepping into your potential. You will never know your potential, until you brave your way, through the thick clouds of fear, to step into the potential. It is from here, that you begin turning your faith into sight. This, however, entails taking a big step of faith, doing something new, going somewhere new, and not cozying in your comfort zone.

If you are a young lady, looking for a husband, and you lock yourself in your home, for a whole year, fasting and praying, you are unlikely to get one, until you step out, to communicate your beauty to a world of bachelors, eager to say, 'I do.' None of the bachelors, willing to marry, will miraculously knock on your door, and say, "I am looking for a wife". No. Ruth didn't do so. She stepped out of her house to the field to meet a husband.

As it is aptly put in James 2: 17, "In the same way, faith by itself, if not accompanied by action, is dead." The American musician, Rich Mullins seemed to have summed up the import of this bible verse, with his "Screen Door" title released in 1987 with the lines: "Faith without works is like a song you can't sing. It's about as useless as a screen door on a submarine." Faith without work is dead, and cannot save you. It is work that ignites and invigorates faith to save.

Though, we are told that work is a punishment imposed on the Adamic race for the sin of Adam, God Himself endured the punishment of work for six days, creating the universe and its constituents. Since God Himself went through the punishment of work, then, that punishment called work, must be an unavoidable ordeal for human survival.

Work, especially hard work, guarantees success and generates respect. More importantly, when you turn your success into a flowing river of charity, irrigating the hope and aspirations of the poor living along its banks, you certainly become a tourism gem, receiving sight and obeisance at all times and in all places. Your presence, everywhere, is a festive occasion, celebrated with pomp; and everyone strives to know you and relate to you.

Hard work makes you grow fitter and better; keeps you positive, motivates you, and gives you the fortitude of self-satisfaction. It makes you enjoy the journey of life and get meaning out of it. Life is not a destination to reach but a journey to travel, and hard work makes this journey interesting and amazing. You enjoy the challenges and landmarks of the journey; you relish your king-size hobbies; you satisfy your self-actualization needs; your confidence level rises, and you achieve the purpose of life.

Deploying your ability to do something, is called work, but it is only when that ability is backed by dedication, determination, and focus, that it becomes hard work. It is this that takes you to the high point of human refinement. It takes more than inspiration to travel to this point. Thomas Edison, the American inventor, who had 1,093 patents, including the lightbulb and phonograph to his name, says, "Genius is one percent inspiration and ninety-nine percent perspiration." And he is driving home the naked truth from experience. Edison made his inventions through the hard work of innumerable trial-and-error experiments.

So, it is with great men and women we celebrate today. Like the farmhand Ruth, who devotedly worked on a rich man's farm to scale to the summit of history, they too labored, perspiring profusely to get to the summit of their chosen fields. The US tennis legends, the Williams sisters, Venus and Serena, built their tennis empire through hard work, practicing and practicing and practicing. At six in the morning, they would be at the tennis court before going to school, and after school, back to the tennis court.

The physicist Albert Einstein was another manifestation of the power of hard work and determination. Unable to speak till the age of four, and dropping out of university with poor grades, with his teacher declaring him a 'never-to-make-it-in-life', Einstein rode on the back of hard work and willpower, taking up several jobs, to become a Physics Nobel Prize laureate in 1921.

Also, Walt Disney, the originator of Disney World. Bankrupt at 22, after a cartoon series failure, and fired by a newspaper editor for lack of creativity, Disney was undaunting, undismayed, and undeterred. He called to play, the propelling forces of hard work and determination, to drive him to create the famous cartoon character, Mickey Mouse. And suddenly, the world was at his feet, hailing and worshipping him. He had created a piece of history.

You too can create a piece of history for the world to applaud you. Hard work always pays off, so, make it your bedfellow. Men and women, who were once written off, and labeled as downgrades of society, hired the services of hard work, under the supervision of faith, to tread the unfamiliar path, to become the brightest stars on the horizons of human progress. You too can engage the services of hard work, and use unwavering faith, as your supervisor, to flog-leap to the top of terrestrial triumph, and be celebrated.

Yes, God lionizes hard work and scorns laziness. This is why most of the personalities in the bible, God called to do His work, were very busy at work, at the very time of their call. Elisha was very busy working when God placed the call of service upon him. He was briskly plowing in the field together with his twelve workers when Elijah threw his cloak upon him, signifying the mantle of succession. Elisha thus, took over from Elijah as God's appointed prophet of Israel on the farm, as he was working.

David was another Bible personality, very busy at work, at the time of his call. A shepherd, as he was, David was dutifully engaged in his routine task of feeding and protecting his father's flocks in the field when he was summoned back home, only to be anointed king of Israel. David was a conscientious worker, carefully guiding, and courageously protecting the flocks, to the extent of even, killing marauding lions and bears with his bare hands.

Moses also received the call of God when he was at work, tending sheep in the desert. Transiting from the royal life in the palace of Pharaoh to ordinary life in the desert, Moses took up a new job of shepherding, a trade universally abominated among Egyptians. And for 40 years, Moses was on the backside of the desert, shepherding his father-in-law's flocks. It was during one of the routine day's works while tending sheep in the desert that, God revealed Himself to Moses in a burning bush, and charged him to deliver the Israelites out of Egyptian bondage.

Gideon as well, was very busy at work when God called him. He was threshing wheat in a winepress, hiding under an oak tree to evade the invading Midianites, when the angel of the Lord appeared to him and revealed to him, a divine military strategy to fight the Midianites. Gideon effectively deployed the strategy, whittling down his 22,000-man force to just 300 soldiers, to miraculously fight and defeat a 135,000-strong Midianite force. Mathematically, every one Israelite soldier confronted and defeated 450 Midianite soldiers, thus, ending the seven-year-long Midian invasion of Israel.

The disciples of Jesus were also hard-working people, most of whom were at work at the time of their call. Four of them - Andrew, Peter, James, and John – were fishermen. Andrew and Peter were fishing when Jesus called them, while James and John were mending their nets at the time of their call. Matthew, a tax collector, was also busy at work in his tax office, collecting taxes, when Jesus called him.

As for Simon the Zealot, he was, indeed, a zealot, a rebel, and a revolutionary. He was an equivalent of Latin America's Simon Bolivar, who in the 19th century, exported revolutions to Colombia, Venezuela, Panama, Ecuador, Peru, and Bolivia, and subsequently led them to independence from Spain. At the time Simon the Zealot received the call from Jesus, he was at work, actively immersed in his nefarious rebel activities, to the extent of even, planning to overthrow the Roman government, under which, Israel was at the time, a colony.

Similarly, Paul was at work when he received the call to follow Jesus. As a lawyer, Paul was driven by the adept knowledge of the law, to persecute followers of Jesus Christ, as he perceived them to be operating against the letter and spirit of the laws of Moses. It was on the journey to Damascus to perform his routine duty of persecuting Christians, that Paul had an encounter with Jesus Christ, and subsequently became a devout apostle of Christ.

God always engages busy people to do His work. He hardly uses lazy people for His assignments. God wants us, to always put to work, the talents He has installed in us, to serve humanity and glorify His name. No matter what we do for subsistence, provided it is legal and conforms to the will of God, we are deploying our God-given talents to work.

Whether we are in a laboratory at Oxford University in the UK, manufacturing the latest drug for the cure of the COVID-19 virus, on a cocoa plantation somewhere in Ghana, gathering cocoa beans, or on a football field in Brazil, playing a football game to win a trophy, we are using our God-given talents to accomplish our assigned tasks. And as we do this, and do it well, we are worshiping God. We are expressing our love to God. Work is a form of worship of God because it fulfills God's purpose for creation. Work prepares and develops the earth for the benefit of humanity and the glory of God.

We should, therefore, not grow weary of work. Work pays, and it pays more when it is applied with dedication, commitment, and focus. Hard-working people are awarded prized possessions because God rewards hard work. Proverbs 1:23 affirms that "In all toil, there is profit, but mere talk tends only to poverty." Ours, therefore, is to find passion in our work and remain steadfast in the Lord. The river of success will ultimately flow on our way.

God so much places a high premium on the role of work in human edification that, the words "labor" and "work" appear more than 480 times in the Bible. When God put

Adam in the Garden of Eden, God instructed him to "work the ground and keep it" (Genesis 2:15). It is interesting to note that, even before Adam and Eve were condemned to "hard labor" for succumbing to temptation and eating the fruit of the forbidden tree of knowledge of good and evil, God had invented the institution of work as the centerpiece of His original plan for humanity. God, the Creator put Adam in the Garden to work and be a co-creator because Adam was made in the image of God, and 'working to create' is a part of God's image.

As bearers or carriers of the image of God, we have the potential to mirror the divine attributes of God and do what God does. God is a hard worker. He worked hard for six long days to create the universe and its constituents and took only a one-day rest. God wants us, too, to work hard and be creators like Him. He wants us to be His co-creators. God wants us to work to discover the earth, work to restore the earth, work to preserve the earth, and more importantly, work to dress up the earth per His prescription in Genesis 2:15.

This is why in Colossians 3:17, Apostle Paul urges us to discharge tasks assigned to us as giving thanks to God the Father. Paul, further, admonishes us in Colossians 3: 23 to perform our duties heartily as if we are working for God and not human masters. For his part, Solomon reminds us in his wisdom-filled book of Proverbs that, "Lazy hands make for poverty, but diligent hands bring wealth" (Proverbs 10:14). Work is very dear to God and God wants us to work to satisfy all our human needs, and glorify Him.

CHAPTER EIGHT

The Unshakable Power of Faith-Shepherded Unfamiliar Path

Commuters on the unfamiliar path subsist on indomitable courage and are compassed by unshakable faith. They see faith as a spiritual treasure whose value cannot be estimated because it has the solution to all problems. For them, faith is the foundation of their very existence. It delivers them anything and everything they desire, provided their desires are within the plan of God. It provides them the insurance coverage for the future. They trust faith to propel them to live the purpose of life.

Unfamiliar-path-bound travelers are so strong-minded about the rewarding powers of faith that they no longer need a lecture or a sermon from anyone, anywhere to convince them. They appear to locate themselves exclusively on the same page with the Italian theologian and philosopher, Thomas Aquinas who stated, "To one who has faith, no explanation is necessary. To one without faith, no explanation is possible."

Those who hold on to faith, trust, and believe God, to care for them. They, therefore, follow God whenever and wherever He leads them. They believe God has perfect plans for them, and that God has built-in mechanisms for the actualization of the plans. They also believe that the actualization mechanisms could be anything and everything. It could, even, be trials and tribulations that would bring untold suffering and hardships. However, they are aware that the trials and tribulations could be intended to discipline and prune them, of sin and help them acquire a Christlike character, to enable them to effectively carry out the assignments, God has for them.

Yes, God always prepares us for every assignment He gives us. Ours, therefore, is to invest our full faith in Him, obey Him, trust Him, and wait on Him, to fulfill His promise. We have nothing to worry about, because Philippians 4:6 counsels us 'not to be anxious about anything,' while 1 Peter 5:7, charges us to 'cast all our care upon Him for He cares for us.'

It is faith, which moves the hand of God, to act. Perhaps, faith is the only currency, acceptable in heaven, for business transactions. Faith is a spiritual currency available to the believer, to purchase anything and everything from God. You can purchase contentment with faith, good health with faith, good education with faith, good marriage with faith, good job with faith, prosperity with faith, salvation with faith; and in fact, all the goods and services available in God's shopping mall of promises. No believer can live joyously without this spiritual legal tender. The currency of faith gives real meaning to the believer's life.

Faith is one of the three avenues of power, that God has made available to believers. The other two are the Holy Spirit and the dominion and authority of Jesus. We have been equipped with these three-layered avenues of power to make us effective witnesses of the Word of God.

The case of faith is unique. There is a direct link between faith and power. The more faith we have in God, the more God directs our lives, and the more power and blessings

He bestows upon us. The tragic absence of faith disrupts the free flow of the power of God because God transmits His power, only when it pleases Him. However, Hebrews 11: 6 states that without faith, it is impossible to please God. When Jesus visited his hometown, Nazareth, "He did not do many mighty works there, because of their unbelief" (Matthew 13:58). It was the lack of faith of Jesus' townsmen and women that undermined the full display of his power in his native home.

Traveling on an unfamiliar path fortified with faith, instills in us, strength, confidence, and bravery. Faith in God, makes us denounce our strengths and rely on the strength of God. It illuminates the pathway for us, in times of darkness, and renews our strength, in times of weakness. Faith in God, builds our confidence, to face and accomplish seemingly impossible tasks. Like the biblical David, faith in God gives us the bravery, to face and defeat the Goliaths, the lions, and the bears in our lives.

In the storms of life, treading the unfamiliar path with faith makes us immovable. We will stand firm like Mount Zion, in the storms of global pandemics, global shortages, soaring inflations, endemic joblessness, social upheavals, and all forms of adversity. Nothing can take away our joy; nothing can steal away our faith, because Psalm 125:1 assures us that, "Those who trust in the Lord are like Mount Zion, which cannot be moved, but abides forever." While the storms are tearing apart homes, workplaces, places of worship, families, communities, and nations, we will stand firm like a rock. Psalm 20 cautions those who repose their security in earthy fortifications like large armies and powerful weapons that, they will be brought to their knees and fall. It, however, assures those who trust in the name of the Lord that, they will stand firm.

Equipped with faith-inspired strength, confidence, and bravery, riders on the unfamiliarity path tend to defy conventionality, and are often, perceived as madmen and women on a provocative mission, to disrupt the tranquil order of tradition, and turn the world upside down. However, it is not so. It is rather through their seeming madness, that light and clarity illuminate the world.

The perceived unfamiliar-path-conformism rebels of yesterday are today, the celebrated front-page innovators, the eminent four-star inventors, and the illustrious major-league discoverers. Their imagination-arresting innovations, inventions, and discoveries are fine-tuning and brightening human civilization. The apparent faith-laden madmen and women plying the unfamiliar path are turning our world 'upside up'.

When the Italian scientist Galileo Galilei wrote in the 17th century that, the Earth and other planets revolve around the Sun, at the center of the universe, he was perceived as a lunatic, bent on unmaking God's ordered world prescribed in the Bible. He was arrested, tortured, tried, and condemned to house arrest, under which he remained, until his death. However, several centuries on, the same 'lunatic' Galileo was celebrated by the scientific world, with the Physics Nobel Prize laureate Albert Einstein, describing him as the "father of modern science."

Unfortunately, truth-seekers in all fields of human enterprise are facing the fate of Galileo. In business, they are wrongly labeled as mutineers and radicals.

Surprisingly, their mutiny and rebellion against conventional principles and practices, are injecting inventiveness and efficiency into hiring. These seeming radicals are critical thinkers, using their self-proclaim radicalism, to markedly differentiate their abilities from the crowd, and gain an advantage over the competition.

Critical thinkers birthing innovations, inventions, and discoveries, are faith-fueled unfamiliar-path voyagers like Ruth. In them, can be found many character traits of Ruth. Like Ruth, they resist traditionalism and tread the unfamiliar path, to look beyond the status quo, to inaugurate new ideas, innovations, inventions, and discoveries. Like Ruth, they have the burning passion and stubborn determination to fire up their dreams to success.

Just as Ruth deployed impeccable work ethics, gleaning in the field of a rich man, innovators, and discoverers exhibit unshakable persistence to weed off challenges that could derail their mission. Acting as Ruth, who took the risk to follow her mother-in-law's instruction to propose to a man with her body, innovators take risks to invest heavily in their new ideas. Like Ruth, who rode on courage to weather the storms of fear, ridicule, and rejection, innovators demonstrate strong courage and willpower to overcome challenges.

The unfamiliar trip of faith always comes with trials, tribulations, and disappointments. However, the faith-laden and faith-propelled story of the biblical character, Job reassures us that 'what does not kill us, makes us stronger. Faithful to the core, and blessed to the brim: plenty of money, happy family, large livestock, loyal friends, good health, and high respect; and suddenly all disappeared. He lost all his money, all his children, all his livestock, all his friends, and all his respect, and his health deteriorated.

Nevertheless, Job did not take the familiar path of apportioning blame for his woes. He took the unfamiliar path of rather, reinforcing his faith in the Lord. And he received a handsome return on his huge investment in faith. God made him stronger, happier, healthier, and wealthier, restoring all his possessions many times than he previously had. This is the commanding power of the unfamiliar path of faith.

Faith is a strong force within us, capable of putting resistance against all forces of fear and dangers haunting us. In faith, we believe and trust that the presence of the omniscient, omnipresent, and omnipotent within us, will steer us through the stormy waters of life. So, we are not deterred from trekking the unfamiliar path. We know God's divine power will carry us through, just as it carried faith-intoxicated Ruth through the stormy waters of her unknown world.

We are told in the Bible that when Moses, an adopted son of a daughter of the king of Egypt, became of age, he treaded the unfamiliar path of faith and refused to be called a grandson of the king (Hebrews 11:24). The decision drove Moses away from comforts of life. He denied himself of the mouth-watering courtesies attached to the powerful Pharaoh's palace: 24/7 security, cozy rides, sumptuous meals, wonderful entertainment, and heart-rendering obeisances.

The act of faith, exhibited here, by Moses, a Jew living inside the power structure of Egypt, is unique. He disowned the Pharaoh family and his Egyptian identity to assume the identity of his biological parents and their nation. He looked beyond his current status as a royal family member, eligible for tempting privileges, to tread the unfamiliar path of faith on a journey to an unknown future.

On the journey of life, there are junctions at which we have to tread the unfamiliar path of faith and deny ourselves of some earthly pleasures to pursue saintly goals. In the case of Moses, we are told, he decided to deny himself of the fleeting pleasures of sin, expressing his preference to be mistreated like other Israelites rather than swimming in a pleasure pool of sins.

We all have our pleasure pools of sin: our lifestyles, our temperaments, our friends, our culture, and our hobbies; the pools are many. We have to identify them and disown them, as Moses disowned the royal Egyptian palace and the Egyptian identity to seek the glory of God. Ruth too did so. She disowned her family and the Moabite society and its pagan gods, to seek the glory of God, and unquestionably accessed it and manifested it.

It is interesting to compare faith-driven Ruth to faith-anointed Abraham, a fascinating character in the Bible, highly revered in Judaism, Christianity, and Islam to be the "Father of Faith". As God called Abraham into the ministry of faith, Abraham left the territory of his faithless extended family in a paganistic Ur city in Mesopotamia and followed the call of God to an unknown land. In the same way, Ruth left her faithless family in paganistic Moab to follow Naomi and the God of unknown Israel, as she was consumed by faith. Both Abraham and Ruth put their trust in God's guidance rather than human devices or human plans or schemes.

Abraham was willing to go wherever God led him, just as Ruth was willing to go wherever Naomi would lead her, saying "Where you go, I will go, and where you stay, I will stay." In their desire to go anywhere and everywhere faith led them, both Abraham and Ruth were not seeking fame and greatness for themselves, but availed themselves to be used as instruments to actualize the plans of God, and bring blessings to humanity.

In his seeming nomadic lifestyle, as he wandered in the land God had promised him, Abraham was willing to allow God to lead him into new relationships. Abraham sought good relations, with those he came into contact with, and built healthy networks with them. In the same way, Ruth was willing to allow God to lead her into new relationships.

Ruth established good working relationships with supervisors of a rich man's farm and the rich man himself, who, subsequently became her husband. Like Abraham and Ruth, we should always endeavor to establish networks and good relationships anywhere and everywhere we find ourselves. It helps build up social capital for enhancing cordial coexistence.

A parallel can also be drawn between Ruth and Rahab, the prostitute who sheltered the two Israelite spies, Joshua sent to scout out Jericho, while the Israelite army was preparing to close in on the city. Both Ruth and Rahab encountered twosome jeopardies of being women and foreigners, as they found themselves posted to the nerve center of the very soul of the Jewish nation. Ruth was a Moabite while Rahab, a Canaanite. Furthermore, Rahab had the jeopardy of a prostitute label embossed on her, while Ruth had the jeopardy of carrying the label of a widow.

Both women had the option of treading the familiar path to follow their nations and their gods or treading the unfamiliar path to follow a foreign nation and a foreign god. But both decided to ignore the lures of their nations and their gods, to tread the unfamiliar path, pitching camp with Israel and its unknown God. Ruth followed her mother-in-law to an unknown Bethlehem, while Rahab heroically, sheltered two enemy Israelite spies, and helped them to escape. Both women did so, under the towering influence of unshakable faith.

Both women were from pagan nations but abandoned their nations and their gods, and followed the God of Israel. Both women practiced to the full, the principle of 'brother's keeper.' Rahab willingly accepted the responsibility for the welfare of the two Israelite spies, while Ruth willingly accepted the responsibility for the welfare of her mother-in-law, Naomi.

Interestingly, Rahab, the harlot married a Jew called Salmon, with whom she gave birth to a son called Boaz, who would become the husband of Ruth, thus making Rahab, a mother-in-law to Ruth (Matthew 1:5). And as fate would have it, the two commonplace, misfortune women of foreign nationalities - the widowed Ruth, a Moabite; and the prostitute Rahab, a Canaanite – both of who had no entrance to a relationship with God, and no claim to the promises of God, became foremothers of Jesus Christ the Messiah.

That is how God weaves the ordinary stories of ordinary people into His bigger stories. Your ordinary story can also become a big story of God. God uses unexpected people, in unexpected circumstances, as unexpected instruments, to propel His expected missions.

Ruth exemplifies the strength of determination, the harvest of commitment and hard work, the reward of obedience, the unlocking keys of hidden potential, the blessings of righteousness, the towering power of faith, and the symbol of abiding loyalty and devotion. Through the joys and tragedies of life: famine, blissful marriage, deaths, widowhood, loneliness, self-exile, beggary job, and re-marriage to bear a son called Obed; God accomplished His plan for Naomi's faithful and dutiful daughter-in-law, Ruth.

And women in Bethlehem were happy for Naomi for having a grandson, and prayed that "the child would become famous everywhere in Israel."

And God answered their prayers, and the child Obed, indeed, became famous in Israel and beyond. He became the father of Jesse, and the grandfather of the famous King David of Israel, through whose lineage, the Messiah, Jesus Christ was born.

God faithfully answered the prayers of the women of Bethlehem, for Naomi. And God hasn't changed and doesn't change. He is the same today, as He was some 32 centuries ago when He answered the prayers of the women of Bethlehem. He is still in the business of answering prayers and will answer your prayers too. Pray. But do so, in faith, with faith, and for faith.

The product of faith is the testimony it produces. Ruth was a product and testimony of faith. You too can be a product and testimony of faith. Hold on, unwaveringly, to your faith, and tread the unfamiliar path. It will, amid the trials and tribulations of our sinful world, lead you to your promised land, for you to manifest the glory of God and be a product and testimony of faith. Pray.

www.ingramcontent.com/pod-product-compliance
Lightning Source LLC
Chambersburg PA
CBHW052150070526
44585CB00017B/2052